Beyond Triathl

A Dual Memoir
of Masters Women Athletes

CELESTE CALLAHAN *AND*
DOTTIE DORION
WITH JANE E. HUNT

Foreword by Sarah Springman

McFarland & Company, Inc., Publishers
Jefferson, North Carolina

This book has undergone peer review.

Library of Congress Cataloguing-in-Publication Data

Names: Callahan, Celeste, 1942– author. | Dorion, Dottie, 1934–
author. | Hunt, Jane E., author.
Title: Beyond triathlon : a dual memoir of masters women athletes / Celeste
Callahan and Dottie Dorion ; with Jane E. Hunt.
Description: Jefferson, North Carolina : McFarland & Company, Inc.,
Publishers, 2021. | Includes bibliographical references and index.
Identifiers: LCCN 2020047112 | ISBN 9781476681702 (paperback : acid free paper) ∞
ISBN 9781476641935 (ebook)
Subjects: LCSH: Callahan, Celeste, 1942– | Dorion, Dottie, 1934– |
Sex discrimination in sports—United States—History. | Stereotypes
(Social psychology) in sports—United States—History. | Women
triathletes—United States—Biography. | Women runners—United
States—Biography.
Classification: LCC GV1060.72.C35 A3 2021 | DDC 796.42092/2 [B]—dc23
LC record available at https://lccn.loc.gov/2020047112

British Library cataloguing data are available

ISBN (print) 978-1-4766-8170-2
ISBN (ebook) 978-1-4766-4193-5

Front cover design by Dottie Dorion and Carlos Carreras Rodriguez
(Twenty First Century Studios)

Printed in the United States of America

*McFarland & Company, Inc., Publishers
Box 611, Jefferson, North Carolina 28640
www.mcfarlandpub.com*

Celeste—
To Dick, my children, and Judy

Dottie—
To My Husband, George, and our family

Table of Contents

Acknowledgments

I thank Dick and my family. Obviously, my life wouldn't have turned out as it has without my husband, Dick. When we had been married just a few years and I was folding the third baby's diapers, I realized I just wasn't in my life and I had no idea how I got there. Later that night, I told my husband I felt like running away. He said, "Make sure you get some good running shoes first." My children only knew me as a runner and triathlete and gave me aero bars when I thought I was done with triathlon. That was when I knew I could keep going with this thing that was just about me.

I want to thank my first two coaches: Todd Starnes in Bellevue, Washington, and Dave Epperson in Denver. Todd took me on in the 1980s, when I was an older athlete at age forty-three. He said just the right words to encourage me. No fluff. Dave Epperson took me on in Denver to help me qualify for the national championships like my Washington friends were doing. He became a good friend as well was a fantastic teacher.

Sarah Springman was one of the first to help me realize that I was an anomaly once I was over fifty. She said at an award ceremony in the Canary Islands that very few athletes on the other side of fifty finish Ironman in thirteen hours. So I began to see that age was a challenge, after all.

Judy Flannery, mentioned so often in this book, was my best friend and I would've followed her anywhere. She just assumed we would keep signing up for races and going to nationals and going to worlds. I was a groupie. Dottie Dorion worked to improve our position in the sport and encouraged other people. She gave me the courage and the support to start my well-known all women's triathlon training group, CWW, in 1997. Two other CWW coaches, Yoli Casas and Julie Lyons, gave me immeasurable tips and advice.

I thank everyone I came in contact with through CWW, especially the women I coached.

Acknowledgments

And I thank everyone I came in contact with, in the sport of triathlon, who helped me to become the athlete and person I am.

—Celeste Callahan

* * * * * *

Family and Friends: George Dorion, my husband, has been my "sponsor" for more than sixty-three years. He has given me the time and support needed to pursue my many dreams. My parents raised and molded me to become the person I am today. We never had a lot of material things, but we never missed them because of a solid and secure family structure. My mom was compassionate and caring for everyone and very artistic. My dad was hardworking and honest. My brothers—my twin Richard, a graphic designer, and Robert, a business school graduate—were like most brothers: there for me but accompanied by lots of teasing and typical fighting over who got the one bathroom first. My grandparents were always "old"—like we are now. They worked hard, especially my Grandfather Simpson, a farmer working 24/7. My grandmothers were always busy without the modern conveniences of today. The canning pantries were filled with home-grown produce thanks to their efforts. Aunts and uncles were always there for family reunions. Our four children and their wives, Mark (Helen), Christopher, Timothy (Sandy) and Lisanne became professionals in a variety of fields, an English teacher, hydrogeologist, physical therapist and attorney. Our three grandchildren represent the next generation of athletes and scholars and continue to inspire me. My mother-in-law was a smart, beautiful lady whom I considered my second mom.

My husband George is my best friend. Friends come in all shapes and sizes and all are treasures because we do not inherit them but choose them for many different reasons to fulfill our lives. We have friends from childhood that we keep forever and others we meet on our walk through life. I have friends from elementary and high school days in Floral Park and Bay Shore, New York. We had neighbors who watched over us in communities where we lived. Laine Silverfield, a bright, discerning and generous friend has been a stalwart in many of my endeavors, always encouraging me. My fellow Osprey Club founders and athletic pioneers at University of North Florida, John Hayt, Tom Healy, Gerry Hurst, Dave Polovina, Dusty Rhodes and the late Doug Harmon all contributed to my drive and confidence—often with humor and challenges. They are my "brothers from other mothers." Also in this category, I thank our executive assistant Marty Cleghorn and finance and insurance coordinator Linda Kurtts for keeping the "Home Front" running smoothly.

Teachers and Coaches: We had teachers who were friends and educated us, helping us grow into respectable human beings. One English teacher at Bay Shore High School taught us how to write and made us diagram sentences for a whole year. Another biology teacher taught us so well that college was easy by comparison! Nursing school at Columbia Presbyterian Medical Center inspired us to the highest standards of our nursing profession and laid the groundwork for what nursing is today. Our instructors, especially Dean Elizabeth Gill, in pharmacology, taught that you are 100 percent right, or you are wrong. Art teachers Allison Watson, Paul Ladnier and Raquel Rodriguez have all taught me and pushed me in developing my painting for more than thirty years.

Coaches were influential in my physical prowess and that started early on, continuing throughout my life. My field hockey coach in high school taught me excellence "On the Field." Later, in triathlon, I had coaches in all three sports—many of them neophytes in the "Tri" sport itself. Hank Lange, a triathlete, coached us older ladies; Jackie Trude taught our "Masters Swim Team"; and Allen Poucher coached me in swimming technique as well. The University of North Florida provided facilities for swim teams and their strength & fitness coach, Vernon Stephens, helped a great deal. Chuck Metzler taught me proper rowing technique. Today many of my friends are coaches as well, especially Kitty Switkes. We can train together all day and admit that it can be one of our best sessions ever. We neither one practice restraint! All of these coaches/instructors are friends.

I thank and acknowledge Sarah Springman for her generous offer to write the foreword. We have known and admired Sarah for decades and are humbled that she would play a part in introducing the book. Dean Kate Moorehead and the clergy staff at St. John's Episcopal Cathedral served as my spiritual coaches. I was also inspired by so many of my friends who joined me in lobbying for laws to be changed so we could establish a nonprofit hospice in Northeast Florida. That effort built my perseverance and has been most successful.

Tribute to Readers of the Book: Reading a manuscript is a labor of love and critiquing a friend's work is never easy. Grateful thanks to Marty Cleghorn, Christopher Dorion, George Dorion, Laurie Kelly, Douglas Mello and Rick Wilson for their assistance and input. Dr. Jane E. Hunt, Bond University, Gold Coast, Australia, is "our narrator" and

Acknowledgments

made this book possible with patience, perseverance, extensive travel and communication while still teaching and researching full time at the University. We are indebted to her and Bond University for letting us borrow her for two years to bring this book to fruition.

—*Dottie Dorion*

* * * * * *

This book is the product of a lifetime of work and energy exerted by Celeste Callahan and Dottie Dorion. It is not the place, here, for me to thank long lists of people. In brief, I would like to express my gratitude to my husband, Shane, and daughter, Josie, for enduring many weeks of my absence without complaint. I thank them also, along with the Faculty of Society and Design at Bond University, for encouraging and supporting me in my desire to bring to print the story of two women for whom sport represented radical resistance to notions of womanhood that inadequately defined them. I must credit Professor Raoul Mortley, in particular, for his interest and timely guidance.

More than anything, I want to thank Celeste Callahan and Dottie Dorion for putting their faith in an unknown researcher from Australia and allowing me to immerse myself in their memoirs and memories. It has been a delightful and rewarding experience.

—*Jane E. Hunt*

* * * * * *

Celeste Callahan, Dottie Dorion, and Jane E. Hunt would like to thank the various photographers who have kindly allowed the inclusion of their images in this book. Despite considerable effort to verify and obtain permission from all photographers, or those holding the rights to the images included in this book, it was not always possible to do so. Should any reader recognize their work and note that they have not been credited for the work, we would welcome the information and gladly arrange for appropriate recognition.

Foreword

Prologue

The third ITU Triathlon World Championships took place in 1991 on the fabled Gold Coast in Queensland, Australia. Yes, really! It was the culmination of a year's focus for elite male and female triathletes and a host of masters triathletes of all ages. I was still competing, just, in the elite category, alongside my voluntary role as co-chair of the ITU Women's Commission. This explains, partially, why I have been asked to contribute this foreword, of which more anon.

I recall writing the key statement in the Women's Action Plan about "Equality of opportunity, recognition and reward for women in triathlon, *with the men*" in early 1990, after the Commonwealth Games demonstration triathlon in Auckland, New Zealand. The ITU Women's Commission hosted its second Women's Conference on the Gold Coast, a few days before the World Championships. It was entitled "Women in Triathlon: Making the Olympic Dream Come True" with our co-chair, Flo Bryan, in the lead.[1]

Members of the World Championship's Local Organising Committee stepped up to raise funds for, and organize, the conference and a

---

1. The conference program included speakers such as 1990 ITU Triathlon World Champion, America's Karen Smyers ("Personal Perspectives on the Sport of Triathlon"), the Chair of Triathlon Australia Women's Committee, Lori Cameron ("Australian Initiatives: A State by State Round Up...."), author Catherine De Vrye ("No Problems, Only Opportunities"), Secretary General of Sweden's National Olympic Committee, Gunilla Lindberg ("Women, Triathlon and the Olympic Movement"), and myself ("The International Perspective: Aims of the Women's Commission"). International Triathlon Union Women's Commission, "Canon Triathlon World Championships Women's Conference—Women in Triathlon: Making the Olympic Dream Come True," 1991 (Sarah Springman Private Collection).

1

sumptuous lunch.[2] We engaged with, and lobbied, our fellow delegates in support of the multiple resolutions we had submitted to the upcoming ITU Congress, to accomplish this much sought after "equality." We tried to achieve this "step by step," so that it was an obvious and fair progression. ITU's Canadian President, Les McDonald, provided much support and encouragement, handing over the floor of Congress for us (me) to chair and lead the debate. All resolutions were passed without any issues.

We had no idea that the masters women competitors had organized to have a breakfast at the same time and that the prime actors in this story, Dottie and Celeste, would also have been in the same town in the same place...

This Book

This is a fascinating story about two "traditional" American wives and mothers, Dottie Dorion and Celeste Callahan, who established their own distinct identities as independent, talented and inspirational women, as they entered the world of masters sport. They joined the running boom initially, and made new athletic and technological breakthroughs in cycling, swimming and particularly in triathlon. These novel experiences allowed them to discover previously hidden talents and their undoubted inner strength, while providing both of them with their own individual journeys that helped them to grow enormously, in a sporting as well as in a personal sense.

Their respective triathlon travels were eventually woven together, through their desire to test themselves on the greatest stages of all: National (U.S.) Triathlon Championships, ITU Triathlon World Championships and the (somewhat inappropriately named) Iron*man* World Championships. Their parallel experiences through a spectrum of "Awakening, Discovery, Empowerment, Embodiment" included many personal challenges. Each of them took on some of the strangest battles that had to be fought, and mostly with victories to show for them. Undoubtedly though, their greatest satisfaction and fulfillment came when they extended their generosity of spirit to helping others to

---

2. Assisted by Jenny McInnes, Lori Cameron et al., with support from the Australian Sports Commission, Queensland's Women in Sport Unit and Triathlon Australia.

achieve their potential, through personal advocacy, creation of new opportunities, building networks and raising money to fund ... mainly, but not exclusively, masters women and others in need.

Meeting both of them at different times, I discovered prior co-location on the Big Island in Hawaii (1985 and 1987 with Dottie, 1988 with Celeste, and then 1989 with both of them) before we were all "in town" for the Gold Coast ITU Triathlon World Championships in 1991. However, we first met properly in Manchester in 1993 (where Dottie organized and her husband, George Dorion, paid for the Women's Masters breakfast, which Celeste attended, and I was invited to join as an underage [under forty years] ITU Vice President). Shortly afterward, Celeste joined my triathlon training camp in Lanzarote in 1994, having just moved to London. I became a witness to their powers of belief, conviction and passion, as both of them charted visionary new ways ahead.

Dottie joined, and subsequently chaired, the ITU Women's Committee and continued as a dynamic advocate for the rights of masters women in the triathlon international governing body, International Triathlon Union (ITU), and her member national federation. She, supported by George, hosted many of the annual Women's Breakfasts at the ITU World Championships, inviting a distinguished speaker each year: an event and form that continues today. She initiated a kit and equipment exchange program called Adopt-a-Triathlete and was vocal on many important issues within ITU. She was deservedly made an Honorary Member of ITU in 2009 (one of only nine awarded in the twenty years since ITU's foundation at that time).[3]

Celeste is proud of her many ITU medal successes, notwithstanding several personal challenges along the way. She started to coach quite early on, inspiring others to explore and extend their personal boundaries, as she had. She qualified as an ITU Technical Official and joined the governance structure of her national federation, USA Triathlon, as a women's representative and as a board member, culminating in the "queenpin" role as secretary general. She won the USA's Judy Flannery Award, recognizing

---

3. Honorary Members: Gunnar Ericsson (IOC), Sweden, 1992; Mr. Sture Jonasson, Sweden, 1995; Dr. Jim Hazel, Australia, 1998; Mr Phil Coles (IOC), Australia, 2000; Dr. Sarah Springman CBE, Great Britain, 2001; Mr. Les McDonald (deceased), Canada, 2008; Mr. Chiharu Igaya (IOC), 2008; Mrs. Anne-Marie Gschwend, Switzerland, 2009; Mrs. Dottie Dorion, United States of America, 2009; Mr. Bill Walker, Australia, 2016. International Triathlon Union, "Honorary Members," last modified February 9, 2017, https://www.triathlon.org/about/honorary_members.

her as an excellent female athlete of high moral character, who gives back to the sport and women in triathlon. She was the inaugural ITU Women's Committee Award of Excellence winner in 2013.[4]

Jointly, Dottie and Celeste were keen to share the challenges that they and other masters women had faced when they embraced triathlon, and particularly those that they had encountered because they were women. It was this desire that led them to embark on this collaborative memoir-writing exercise. As a cultural historian interested in women and sport, and triathlon in particular, Dr. Jane E. Hunt's research fortuitously brought her into contact with Dottie and Celeste, just as they had completed the first draft of their respective manuscripts. What a thrill it must have been for her to be able to dive into these highly original memoirs!

Jane has acknowledged the difference between their experiences and her own, as a younger Australian woman. She treats their accounts as constructed narratives on their lives as pre–Title IX masters women athletes and tries to understand their experiences more fully by reflecting on what Dottie and Celeste choose to say and not to say, and how they say it. As a result, she could conclude that both Dottie and Celeste are committed to the long-term goal of gender equality in sport in their own way.

The world of masters triathlon is significantly better off for their past efforts, and for their willingness to write about their experiences. We can learn much from these two wonderful role models and the stories they have chosen to share. I can only encourage you to read this book! The pages almost turn by themselves. This book is an eye-opener. You will be inspired.

Sarah Springman, OBE, CBE, competed in the first triathlon in Britain (1983), won eleven national titles, three European titles, and five European team golds and finished top five at the Ironman World Championships. She held Women's Triathlon Training camps from 1985, co-chaired the inaugural International Triathlon Union (ITU) Women's Commission (1989), served as ITU Vice-President (1992–1996, 2008–2016) and as British Triathlon Federation President (2007–2012), and lobbied for Olympic, Paralympic and Commonwealth Games status for triathlon. Professionally, she has served as a professor for geotechnical engineering from 1997, and rector from 2015, at ETH Zurich.

---

4. Doug Gray, "Women's Committee Award of Excellence: The Legendary Figures Honoured So Far," International Triathlon Union, May 1, 2018, https://www.triathlon.org/news/article/womens_committee_award_of_excellence_the_legendary_figures_honoured_so_far.

Introduction:
Unanswered Questions

Astonishing, really—watching old women cry. The two women stare, fixated, at a television on the wall. One cradles a box of Kleenex; the other slumps into the depths of a dusk red lounge. The image contradicts what I had begun to know of them: two cultural icons and, well, pioneers, in a sport rumored inaccurately to have begun as a Honolulu bar room bet.

A contact first suggested that I talk to Dottie Dorion and Celeste Callahan in 2015, as I embarked on a two-armed cultural history project. I was interested in the impacts of Title IX—the 1972 provision for gender equality at government-funded American educational institutions—on women's experiences beyond college and professional sport. The ranks of women runners began to grow in the same decade and the first modern triathlon took place in southern California in 1974, with women participants among the very first cohort of multisport athletes. From previous research I suspected that triathlon—which combines swimming, cycling and running—represented the next challenge for women enjoying the new adventure of athleticism. In addition, triathlon by reputation has a strong track record on gender equality. So the second arm of my project related to the case study of triathlon. I was interested in the possible convergence of post–Title IX opportunities for women to experiment more freely with sport, and the consolidation of the seemingly woman-friendly sport of triathlon.

During my 2015 research trip, I met Dottie and Celeste separately— Dottie in Vermont, aged eighty-two; and Celeste in a hotel room in San Francisco, aged seventy-two. Dottie had recently won her age group at the indoor rowing world championships. Celeste was apprehensive about an event in which she had registered to participate the following day—a swim from Alcatraz to Eastern Beach. I had no idea that Dottie and Celeste knew each other, were good friends, and a year earlier began to

5

document their roles in the multifaceted campaign to increase the participation of women in triathlon worldwide. The timing of my visit seemed fortuitous.

I returned home to Australia armed with their draft memoirs—intended for co-publication—and copious notes of my own. My job was to shovel a path forward, to work out where the path should go.

The task was made difficult because neither provided a complete account of their experiences, or expounded on what each had done. In their memoirs Dottie and Celeste devote more time to their respective transformations from mothers who played social tennis into women who competed for race medals, than to their impressive achievements. They are modest—even off-hand—in mentioning their accomplishments. I learned from Celeste that Dottie was particularly skilled as a skier, something the latter did not mention once in writing or conversation. And Celeste mentioned her own participation in the team cycling event Race Across America in half a sentence. She did it three times!

So, two years later I sit in the lounge room of Celeste's home at Naples, Florida, watching Dottie and Celeste as they watch a documentary called Judy's Time.

Judy Flannery was a central figure in the busy and fulfilling triathlon lifestyles Dottie and Celeste enjoyed from the mid–1980s. Judy died in a cycling accident on April 2, 1997. Her loss was, as Celeste put it, "catastrophic." It was felt not just by the two women sitting opposite me, but by thousands of triathletes all over the United States who pattered like ducklings after the athletic, gregarious, compassionate fifty-seven-year-old mother of five. Erin, the eldest of Judy's children, was at film school at the time. In her grief she produced an award-winning documentary about her mother. It touches on many aspects of the journeys undertaken by masters women triathletes like Dottie, Celeste, and Judy, as well as Judy's wish to see more women become involved in the sport.

Of course, Dottie and Celeste viewed the film many times before we gathered at Celeste's Naples home. But I asked to watch the documentary together with them, in part because I wanted to see whether they express memories and emotions differently when they are not thinking about potential readers.

The scene before me affirms the reality of the grief expressed in their memoirs. But I realize also that their Judy stories are not about loss and sorrow. When Dottie and Celeste write about her, Judy almost appears as a symbol. They use the word "Judy" both to denote a much-loved mutual friend, and to define particular types of "work" as well as specific periods in their lives. The documentary's title, Judy's Time, *is apt. As I reflect on it, the name "Judy" seems like code for something that Dottie and Celeste understand implicitly, but as yet remains unknown to me.*

The thought intrigues me; it feels like I have found a signpost for a trail to a lookout in the distance. It invites me to plunge into—what is for me—an unexplored wilderness. Dottie and Celeste share memories that took shape against the cultural backdrop of mid–twentieth century young adulthood and motherhood. To see the landscape as they see it, I need to follow their narrative trails.

But there is no map for this wilderness, or the trails that Dottie and Celeste explore. Instead they scatter clues, to tell me where they have traveled. As Celeste explains in her memoir:

Carrying on with the story of my life is beginning to sound like the reciting of the rosary. There is going to be a point some time, but maybe it won't come till we've plowed through quite a few. Points, that is.

Conversing separately with Dottie a day or so before we all gathered at Naples, I asked about the way in which her memoir slides between the past and present, to which she responded:

I think that when I take a grand finale event and we start talking about that, I have to back track to connect some dots to get to the end point.

Now, as I recognize the symbolism of the word "Judy," I wonder whether Celeste's "points" or Dottie's "dots" might be more than simply the details they share about the past, but rather anecdotes, images, people, or words they use to evoke the past in specific and meaningful ways. I have a feeling that these clues, like pink ribbons tied to tree branches leading trail runners to the race finish, will help me to navigate the narrative trails of their memoirs.

Judy's Time *ends. The tissue box sits on the coffee table. We sip iced tea. The next item on my itinerary for the afternoon is "joint interview with Dottie and Celeste." Having spent days interviewing them separately, I mean for the group discussion to provide spontaneous accounts of the past, and—I hope—to cast their shared experiences in a different light. From what I have learned about the two women before me, I expect the conversation to be entertaining.*

Before posing my first question for the afternoon, I hesitate. Instead of launching into the weighty topic of the project's aim—Dottie's "end point"—I decide to start with an obvious, easy question; a small detail overlooked: "When did you first meet?"

Introduction

Dottie shifts her slight body back in the lounge, lost momentarily for words. Celeste ruffles her hair. Silence ensues. Celeste responds eventually:

It's significant that we can't remember meeting each other.... I did Portland.

Dottie:

I did Hilton Head.

I know enough to realize that "Portland" and "Hilton Head" are code words as well. Tied to these place names are myriad "flashes of memory," as a historian referencing Walter Benjamin once put it.[1] In this instance, the flashes of memory relate to sporting events. Several hundreds of people might share memories of the 1987 National Triathlon Championships at Hilton Head, but the place name also evokes inevitably something that is specific to the experience of each person who was there. The meanings that Dottie and Celeste attach to the code word of "Hilton Head" are both similar and different.

There is one commonality at least: "Hilton Head" does not evoke memories of meeting each other.

Finally, Celeste directs herself to Dottie:

Maybe I met you in '89 at the women's breakfast.

In her memoir Dottie mentions attending "breakfast" prior to her first ultradistance triathlon. Known colloquially as "Ironman," the ultra-distance triathlon is still held in October at Kailua-Kona on Hawaii's Big Island every year. When Dottie qualified for Ironman in 1985, she traveled to Kona a few weeks early so that she had time to train and overcome her nerves.

It was a very new experience for me. I felt very apprehensive.

When I went down to "Dig Me" Beach at Kona to look at where we had to swim, it was with fear and trepidation. At first, I felt very intimidated by all the people there, so I was excited to see other women like me.

One of them invited the small cohort of over-forty women competitors to her home for breakfast, as Dottie explains:

Our first masters breakfast was held at Janet's home up in the mountains. The breakfast was a heartwarming occasion to honor the older women pioneers in the sport.

---

1. Douglas Booth, "Escaping the Past? The Cultural Turn and Language in Sport History," *Rethinking History* 8, no. 1 (2004): 120.

More breakfasts ensued over the years. Dottie links their importance to the growing confidence that she and other attendees gained from sharing their athletic journeys:

We all gave each other reassurance and became such good friends. I still stay in touch with several of them. We went to the jeweler and got an Ironman ring. Whenever we were in a difficult situation, we would touch our Ironman ring. It gave us courage and a sense of leadership, and all sorts of major qualities that we needed in special moments. I got into a few heated discussions and I would do that, I would look at my Ironman ring and it gave me the fortitude to go on—if you can do an Ironman you can do anything. We felt that it really made us strong—mentally, spiritually, and physically.

Dottie participated in the Bud Light Ironman Triathlon World Championships in 1985, and in 1987 and '89, but she was not there when Celeste first attended in 1988. Before Dottie arrived for our gathering at Naples, Celeste told me about her first "breakfast" over—ahem—breakfast.

When I qualified for Ironman in 1988, someone said that I should go to the women's breakfast. She said it was the most important thing I could do.

Just two dozen or so women gathered for the earliest breakfasts, but by 1988 it was so large they held it at Kona Hotel and charged $18 a head. It was on a Thursday morning, and I remember I had a flat tire when I drove my rental car down Ali'i Drive. There were three Hawaiian men there. I said to them, "$10 if you can fix it in ten minutes." Done!

It was extremely emotionally important to be with women that old, over forty—pre–Title IX women—going to the breakfast. It was the first time I met other competitors and talked to them. They just accepted you. They sat around the table and talked, many for the first time ever, about themselves—not about their children. They were spoken *to* as themselves—not as wives of the men who'd bought the plane ticket to get them there.

We were all of the same persuasion. All were displaced homemakers, all homemakers who wanted to do something else. We all wanted to do something different to the men who take care of us—"I'm here representing me."

We were in Kona to participate in an event for which we alone had qualified, that we alone would do, and, for the first time we began to see ourselves with boundaries—where we ended and someone else began. It meant so much to me to be visible as a person.

9

Introduction

What I liked; I had all these friends who saw me as me. I had always been daughter, mother, wife. The identification thing was critical.

While Dottie was not at the breakfast in 1988, Judy was. As Celeste explained to me, she first spoke to Judy en route to Kona:

I saw her the next morning and I saw her at the breakfast. I had a rental car and asked if she wanted to drive the bike course with me.

And that was that.

With the dusk red lounge transforming into a silhouette, backlit by the last shards of afternoon light, Celeste emphasized, once more, the importance of breakfast:

The women's breakfast was the start of a lot, a lot of things.

"Breakfast—code word," I scrawl on my notebook page in the half light. Bound up with the word, seemingly, is a feeling—a poignant realization on the part of women for whom the possibilities of Title IX held little direct relevance because they had graduated years earlier—that the personal challenge of triathlon gave them membership to a global athletic community and a passport to a reality that contradicted conventional expectations.

I have more questions about "breakfast." We have not established when Dottie and Celeste first met. And I still do not know exactly the "end point" of the memoirs drafted by Dottie and Celeste. But we are tired. Dottie, Celeste and I disperse to rest, or run, or refresh ourselves, with none of my questions answered.

After days of sorting through boxes of old photographs and race results, chuckling at event tee shirts in every shade of neon, and interviews in which more questions seem to be raised than answered, I take my seat on a flight out of Fort Myers. It is not that Dottie and Celeste did not try to respond to my questions, but each answer seemed to take me further into unknown territory. I take out my notebook and reflect on the growing list of code words—"Hilton Head," "Wilkes-Barre," "Judy," "breakfast" and many others. I circle them and draw lines around and between them. The aimless lines remind me of where I started when I first thought of "Judy" as a code word, the idea of the narrative trail.

Initially Dottie and Celeste used the metaphor of airplane travel to structure their memoirs, with "Contents May Have Shifted" as the original title. By the time I sat down with them at Naples, they had rejected the idea. I welcomed the decision. Built into the idea of flight on a commercial airline is a whole set of expectations—there is a set destination, and rules and conventions aimed at controlling the way that passengers move and behave. This might be analogous to the conditions described in the opening chapters of the memoirs drafted by Dottie and Celeste, but in the stories that they tell about their sporting lives, they defy expectations. They do not follow a travel itinerary—they choose their own paths. And now they want to tell others about their unconventional journeys and what they have learned along the way. Like their sporting lives, the memoirs do not follow rules. The paths—or trails—are unfamiliar. Dottie and Celeste highlight landmarks and leave clues—like the code words—inviting their readers to follow and to see what they see.

So I start to list clues on a clean page, and draw lines between them again. But this time I am more purposeful. What do I need to know before I can understand this or that code word? Quickly the page is transformed as I scribble snatches of words and phrases, until I have a sequence of clues that each appears to represent the heart of a possible chapter.

Recognizing that I am inserting myself into the narrative, I decide to do so openly, to use italicized text to separate the navigational aids I add from the memoirs. I also decide to start the dual memoir with a glimpse of Dottie and Celeste as triathletes, before backtracking like Dottie does in her oral and written anecdotes, to join the dots that led to this point. When they write about childhood Dottie and Celeste reveal the outline of the landscape that shapes their respective stories. While Dottie frames her memories of childhood in terms of vulnerability, hard work and freedom, Celeste writes about anxiety and control. Expectation looms on the horizon of both stories. Because they were girls, they were taught to behave in specific ways, and to hope for specific things.

Chapter two features the memoir narratives about young adulthood. Dottie and Celeste appear to fulfill all that they were taught to expect of womanhood. They marry hard-working men and start to raise families. But the chapter concludes with the feeling implicit in both memoirs that something is missing, an uneasiness that both women express in their accounts of social tennis. Social tennis seems like code for a point that Dottie and Celeste are trying to make about the way in which they, and women like themselves, had been taught not to embrace sport and life in the same way as men. Against this backdrop, their tales of transformation into runners (in chapter three), marathon runners (in chapter four), and subsequently into triathletes (in chapter five) appear as stories of radical departure.

I pause. What now? Athletic transformation is not the "end point." In fact, it almost seems like the very start of the trail marked out by Dottie and Celeste. A significant clue seems to lie in Dottie's account of her first Ironman triathlon at Hawaii in 1985. It was meaningful, but that was where Dottie attended the first masters women's breakfast. As a code word "breakfast" seems potentially more meaningful than "Ironman." There was chapter six.

For Dottie and Celeste, the next decade or so featured a range of athletic challenges, leading Celeste to characterize this phase in terms of continuously "stepping up." Yet chapter seven is less about specific multisport undertakings than the consolidation of the continuous cycle of training and competition as active lifestyles.

As Dottie and Celeste recount countless athletic adventures, it becomes clear that they are not alone. Other women, like the women they met at breakfast, wander in the wilderness with them. Many of them also grew up in the shadow of expectation. In chapter eight I see them all slashing pathways through the scrub as they discover and conquer new athletic challenges. The trails begin to converge. Dottie and Celeste finally write about each other, and Judy appears as a central figure. Judy encourages many of them to think about their individual athletic pursuits in terms of the progress of their sex. Triathlon is not simply taking shape around the breakfast women. The shape of the sport is determined in part by their presence.

As used by Dottie and Celeste, the word "Judy" appears to also symbolize their own work to involve more women in triathlon (and sport more broadly). Chapter nine combines Celeste's memoir and oral accounts about the "busy work" she conducts, catalyzed by Judy's tragic passing in 1997. Celeste's "Judy work" begins with the founding of an all-women triathlon training squad and leads to her membership of the executive board of the sport's national federation, USA Triathlon. Chapter ten reveals Dottie as a woman who first sets out to "change the culture of things" shortly after she takes up running. In the 1990s, during the same years that she, Celeste, Judy, and many other women compete in iconic triathlons around the world, Dottie's work shifts to focus more directly on women and sport. She creates a new breakfast tradition at the International Triathlon Union's annual World Championships and a newsletter for masters women around the world, serves as a member of the International Triathlon Union Women's Committee, and campaigns for Title IX compliance in Florida.

The clues and connections are less clear in the closing pages of the memoirs drafted by Dottie and Celeste. Both position themselves in the recent past and reflect on the respective journeys they have taken, although there is not yet a feeling that they have arrived at the "end point." Among the varied reflections is some commentary on their bodies, a subject that is largely absent in the rest of the memoir narratives. Chapter eleven, I decide, should engage with this new angle, which emerges as Dottie and Celeste focus on aging and its impacts on their athletic pursuits. Diminishing athletic capacity prompts Celeste to re-inscribe "stepping up" as a code word. Originally, "stepping up" provided a way to compensate for the handicap of being a girl and a mother in an age when those conditions were viewed as antithetic to the meanings embedded in the code word of "sport." In its new usage, "stepping up" refers to the successive age groups in which Celeste competes, and her emerging role as a symbol of active old age. Age clearly has something to do with the stories that Dottie and Celeste tell, but it seems that for Celeste gender is a more central issue. Dottie embraces her role as model of healthy old age more readily but indicates that the subject still does not represent the "end point." If anything, it almost seems like a tangent, a deviation from the point.

It is significant to me that at the conclusion of her narrative Dottie overtly tries to extract lessons from her journey, many of them about the value of being physically active, and many others about the value of the work that she and other women have done to make sport more inclusive of women. Her comments feel neither like self-congratulation nor a "grand finale." It feels more like she is trying to show that the conventions that shaped her life when she was a child and young adult are a part of the past, that she is describing a changed landscape, and proposing a new set of expectations for younger women and girls. In a way, Celeste's closing thoughts do the same thing. It almost feels like the "end point," but not quite.

As I grapple with the problem of where the memoirs end, the words on the page begin to blur, disintegrating into random scribbles; fragments, disconnected and meaningless. The hum of the airplane engine is lulling me to sleep.

I pull myself back to the question of the "end point," recalling Celeste's rosary:

There is going to be a point sometime, but maybe it won't come until we've plowed through quite a few. Points, that is.

I feel like I have found quite a few points, but not THE point. Dottie and Celeste have shown me the landscape of their youth, how it shaped them, how sport has helped them to transform, and how they in turn have transformed that landscape. They have shown me a new and enticing vista, but not the end point.

Resisting sleep, I realize with a jolt that Dottie and Celeste cannot tell me the end point, because we are not there yet. They are pointing ahead and telling me, telling us, that the end point is still somewhere out there. They want us to keep on moving forward, to find the answers for ourselves.

With this revelation I do not have a new truth as such, but I do have resolution.

I let myself slide toward slumber. The search for answers will have to wait.

1

Rope Swings and Grasshoppers

Dottie:
I started this thing called "triathalon" in 1980. I didn't even know how to spell it.

Celeste:
"Is this your first triathlon?" said the woman standing in the reeds next to me. My idea was to stand until the gun went off and then run into the water—not tread till my feet turned blue. I was not alone in that thought. I had told my husband to come during the run. My nightmare was my hyperventilating in front of him and being pulled out of the lake. The gun went off.

So I swam. I have no idea how long I took. I know I was not last. I went in the change tent to put on a run outfit. With bra. I took fourteen minutes that day. I rode a girl's bike—it had a basket on the front—with a quarter in my shoe in case I had a flat tire. I saw the leaders, men, coming back from wherever we turned around. I finished the bike. I was thrilled. I had not drowned; I had not had a flat tire. That they were taking down the gantries did not faze me. The run was horrible until mile two. Then I flew. I finished with five people behind me. But I didn't care. My prize was hearing the booming voice of the official: "Only triathletes in the transition area," as I went to get my gear. I guess I was a triathlete. The sky was a darker gray now. But I have never seen the sky so bright.

Dottie Dorion and Celeste Callahan were not destined to be triathletes. Nothing in their stories about childhood indicate that their paths would lead them to triathlon, or that they would be part of—and help to usher in—radical change in the sporting lives of women across the world.

Nor is there any sign in their accounts of childhood that someday their paths would cross. Older by eight years, Dottie was born on February 19, 1934, and raised in the Northeast of the United States. Born August 29, 1942, in the Deep South, Celeste spent portions of her

15

childhood and teenage years in Germany, Spain and other parts of the United States.

Dorothy Mae Simpson grew up in a world recovering from the Great Depression and hurtling toward another world war. As the child of middle-class parents living on Long Island, New York, none of that appears to have troubled her directly, but it manifests occasionally in family endeavors etched into her memory and deemed worthy enough to note in her memoir:

That little girl with pigtails was born a preemie with her twin brother. Together we weighed less than a five-pound bag of sugar. Fortunately, we were born in a snowstorm in February and the electricity was out for several days. We weren't given one hundred percent oxygen, which was a common [*and flawed*] procedure in the '30s. This saved us from becoming blind. Fed with a medicine dropper and packed in a bassinette with hot water bottles, we got off to a shaky start to life.

Although we grew up on Long Island my parents were Vermonters who worked hard their entire life. We moved to "the sticks"—Long Island—and that gave us much more open space. We had a good family life.

My dad commuted to work with Ma Bell [*a term used for the Bell System of telephone companies*], and "brought home the bacon." He knew the names and family members of everyone who worked for him at the telephone company. An accomplished track and field athlete, he developed a new technique for javelin throwing while at the University of Vermont—he would throw it lower. I got into track as a kid because I used to practice throwing broomsticks. I also threw javelin as a masters athlete, after we moved to Jacksonville.

My mom was a home economics school teacher at Bay Shore High School; compassionate and caring, teaching living skills to "challenged" students. And she taught boys, even football players, how to cook. No teacher in high school wanted "hall" duty except by the home economics room. The aromas of cooking wafted the halls: pizza, cakes and cookies, and if you were good you might get a sample—even at 8:00 a.m.! My mother made all my clothes and to this day it is exciting to actually buy clothing.

No parents are ever perfect. But my parents tried. Both were first time college graduates in their families. My dad took a year off from school when their barn burned down and he and his father rebuilt it. My mom left home at an early age escaping from an abusive situation and worked her way through school by housekeeping and cooking. I never heard my mom complain about washing cloth diapers, putting them through a ringer and hanging them on the clothesline. They were huge influences in my life as are all parents, or as all parents should be.

Our family set responsibilities for us to complete chores each week; some were mundane, some were not. A "fringe" from my dad's job was the delivery of old telephone poles for us to cut and split for firewood. This was the hardest wood in the world and the big day came when we finally got a two man saw.

My entire life, I was actually running. I was very busy with my twin brother. As twins growing up, we were very energetic, mischievous and probably today we would have several "tags" on us for these characteristics. But it was just normal. Little kids should be running and playing jump rope.

We just played all day, no equipment necessary. Usually a ball of some kind was available, or a bat and ball. Yeah, it was nice to have a park or playground thrown in every now and then, or maybe visit a country fair or a circus, or pay your five cents to a traveling merry-go-round that came to the neighborhood. Big treat afterwards was the Good Humor truck and just waiting for the day you found a Lucky Stick and got a free ice cream. Sometimes we had a special treat. We had a neighbor who had an above ground pool or

Jump rope was among Dottie's favored activities as a child in the 1930s (Dottie Dorion Collection).

Dottie and her twin brother Richard (Dick), riding horses at their grandparents' farm in the 1930s (Dottie Dorion Collection).

a rope swing with a suspended old car tire for our seat that we could play on, if we were good. Summers we spent on my grandparents' farm, where all of our hyperactivity was put to good use: milking, haying, bothering farm animals, fishing, and chores.

When air raids began after Pearl Harbor our "normal" lives were put on hold to support the war effort. Dad was an air raid warden, Mom knitted non-stop (remember those gloves without thumbs or index fingers so they could shoot?), I passed cookies at the U.S.O. [*United Services Organization*], and we all worked our "Victory Gardens." We carefully saved our ration books, collected milkweed pods, saved aluminum foil and cans of grease and patched our tires and resoled our shoes. We all listened intently every night to follow the path of the war and what a great way to learn geography. Afterwards, lying with our ears glued to the big console radio we had our Armstrong decoders ready for the latest secret messages from Jack, "the All American Boy."

Sometimes the wheels of progress move slowly. We gradually evolved to a country where equipment became necessary to meet the demands of sports. I remember one Christmas when I wrote my letter to Santa and all I wanted was a pair of figure skates. Christmas morning came and there were my brand new, white figure skates. I couldn't wait to try them on. I put on my skate socks and slipped my foot into one skate. The skate was huge, and my toes were two inches away from the tip. My dad said, "I got them a big size so you could grow into them." I skated with my new skates packed with paper in the toes. My feet never grew any longer.

Of course, the equipment was archaic. Skiers, could you ever imagine wooden skis, bamboo poles and hiking boots? And skiing in blue jeans and a windbreaker? Runners had black spike track shoes to run on cinder tracks. Yoga was a distant future and so was triathlon. When I was a youngster playing tennis, the progression started with an old wood racket, Don Budge on the handle. It went bye bye to be replaced by a Bancroft racket. Next came a Head metal racket. And, think about swimming. I had a bathing suit that covered most of my upper body and a little flounce skirt down to mid-thigh—definitely not a sex symbol.

Children—people—select memories for telling and re-telling, for a variety of reasons. Dottie and Celeste not only share something about what they thought and did as children, they also describe aspects of their childhood that were meaningful then and retained relevance over time. They invite the reader to join the dots and follow the narrative trail into the forest of the child's mind.

In her accounts of childhood Dottie juxtaposes vulnerability and freedom. She and her twin brother quickly left their shaky start behind them and appear to have enjoyed a relatively carefree and active childhood. The image of a pig-tailed girl playing on a rope swing somehow seems to embody this sketch of an idyllic childhood characterized by freedom and movement. The onset of war introduced a new form of vulnerability to the childhood that Dottie recalls, but she defrays the darkness of war with recollections of patriotic activities. As she directs the reader along her narrative trail, she points to the light filtering through the leaves above, rather than the shadows at her feet.

Celeste's journey began at around the same time that Dottie and her brother listened to the radio, following dutifully the war's progress. But for Celeste the war was not something experienced from afar and second hand, an imagined terror wrought by machines and mythologized heroes and villains. War crafted not just the backdrop, but the storyline of Mary Celeste Burke's earliest years:

My parents were from Southwest Louisiana, each side of the family rooted in the same spot since the pre-colonial days. Hubris and *noblesse oblige* molded me as though I were of clay.

Beyond Triathlon

I was born into a world in turmoil at Kirtland Air Force Base in Albuquerque. I grew up on Air Force Bases all over the country.

As she recalls it, Celeste's father boasted an impressive resume:

My father, named Dracos Dimitry—he wouldn't wish that name on anybody—decided to join the Air Force, unvelcroing himself from New Iberia. He told me recently that when I was born, he gave a cigar to his flight mate Jimmy Stewart—a famous actor. My father was a bombardier, and eventually an instructor in use of Norden bombsights. After the war he discovered that he instructed one of the bombers of the *Enola Gay* that led to the surrender of Japan. When I was four, he was transferred to Germany and able to watch the Nuremberg trials.

When the war ended, my father went to law school and climbed the ladder to become Judge Advocate of the Strategic Air Command by the time he retired to Louisiana. There, he was offered a position as acting District Attorney. His signature case was made into a movie—*Dead Man Walking*. He assigned a death penalty and it gained attention.

My mother, Carrie Dupuy Burke, was twenty years older than me, a stay at home mother who didn't finish college. She was a busy mother managing a large young family during the war. She told me that if anything happened to my father, she would have to scrub floors.

My early memories are laced in anxiety. Recollections include—this just before departing for Germany—a grasshopper *bigger than the house* standing right behind me and my father's not looking up from his paper to open the back door to my incessant cries; a mid–Atlantic breakdown of the SS *Tyler* that took women and children to join the men and my watching my mother learn how to smoke; my mother's warnings that I was never to take anything to eat from any German, but, if offered, to run home as fast as I could.

Once I was sitting on the wall that surrounded our building and found I could not get down. Recognizing the American uniform on a gentleman passing by, I asked him to help me. He did. I ran to tell my mother about the nice man. To say that she lost it is an understatement, and I learned that, if a man ever put me in a sack and carried me away, I was to kick and scream. Makes for a good night's sleep—that—when you are four.

Where Dottie points upward and outward, Celeste points downward to the darkened earth beneath the undergrowth in the forest of childhood memories, but there are occasional parallels in their narratives.

Embedded in the memoirs drafted by both Dottie and Celeste— as well as in their responses to my subsequent questions—are a series of lessons drawn from their childhood experiences. They are like the times table, told as if rote learned rather than the product of frustration, anguish or pragmatism. Their stories belie the length of time it took to gain perspective on the invisible forces that nudged them along a pre-determined path.

Celeste:

That both my parents were from as far south as one can go in Louisiana and pride themselves on having family from before Louisiana became a state and both grandmothers were Daughters of the American Revolution, was important in the way I was raised. I had a responsibility to uphold. I was not. I belonged. I was less than was "we."

While Celeste may have been terrified of an imagined over-sized grasshopper, she does not appear to be daunted by the height or steep slope of this slide as a child in the mid–1940s (courtesy Dracos Burke).

In the '40s, success was measured in how well one kept from calling attention to oneself. When I got to school toward the end of the decade, we wore uniforms, and, of course, the nuns (that I am Roman Catholic is part of my background) all looked alike. On summer days, we were to appear at supper exactly as we had appeared at breakfast—the way our mothers dressed us—but with no added soil or wrinkled cotton sashes. My parents had a philosophy that a good journey meant one without mishaps. "Adventures make you late for dinner," my mother would quote the Hobbit.

Mine was a life of just missing the mark. My grades in Deportment were always gold stars but I was a decent B student as nothing but languages was easy for me. Multiplication tables did not make sense to me

Celeste (right), with her brother Michael and mother Carrie Burke, enjoying sled rides while her father was stationed in Germany for the Nuremberg trials in the mid–1940s (courtesy Dracos Burke).

and, still today, conjure up memories of middle-aged nuns jumping from behind doors, shouting things like "Six times seven." So I shut down in the math department.

I knew how to study, though, and I knew how to please the teachers. In my senior year of high school, the physics nun approached me to say I had failed miserably the final exam. I was in the Honor Society, so wanting was South Carolina in people who were short. She whispered, looking left and right, that if I promised to tell no one, she would tutor me and give me the test again. She did. I assume I passed.

I do remember I became engaged in a lot of "I Speak for Democracy" contests—this was during the Cold War. I remember one night the parish priest came over to help my dad direct me in a bit. The latter wrote, beginning with "In the spring of 1912, the finest luxury liner afloat…." Not having thought about this evening in almost sixty years, I cannot imagine why the priest was there. My father never did my homework for me, so this instance remains a mystery. I just remember that my best was always expected, if not delivered.

When we were stationed in Spain and I was fourteen years old, I was recommended by the school principal to audition for a part in David Lean's "Fifteen Mysteries of the Rosary." My father actually levitated. I met with the director. I was asked to return. I was given the script. When I went back a week later, I knew the script by heart. Thanks, Dad. Mr. Lean said I was the first actress he had ever met who had memorized the script by main interview. I got the job.

Although she was expected to avoid adventures, the scraped knee and dirty shins in this photograph of Celeste as a child in the mid–1940s suggests that she did not always comply with expectation (courtesy Dracos Burke).

As I look back, though, I cannot think of anything that distinguished my life from any other until I was in my, oh, late 30s. Once, at six, I was asked to go up to the eighth grade to recite "Little Boy Blue" by Eugene Field. My father, as well as his mother, had been keen on elocution. But that was it. The Good Girl (I was the oldest of five—and then, when I was fourteen, oldest of six), I just did what I was told. Or, better said, what was expected of me.

One time, I peed in the garden, an event with repercussions that, fifty years later, would make me famous with the female triathletes of Colorado. Besides not to relieve myself outdoors, I learned, back Stateside, to be quiet because Daddy was always studying for Law School. I learned not to undress my Tony doll in front of the boy across the street. And from my mother, a fan of irony who could pick up house on a dime and move us, a small baseball team, across the world while making clothes and serving dinner, that helplessness was a lifestyle that I was to embrace in order to find someone to marry me, to take care of me. The implication was that I could not take care of myself.

Though she says so in less direct terms, Dottie also understood that her options were limited:

In grade school I had a problem since I was left-handed and my teacher tied that hand behind my back so I would be right-handed like everyone else.

At Bay Shore High School, Long Island, in the '50s, I participated in gym and a variety of sports daily. I was encouraged to do cheerleading, but I only did it for one year. Instead I started to take on leadership roles in the student government and as captain of a big Sport's Night competition between two teams.

I had three courses of study to choose from: secretarial, technical or college entrance (nurse or teacher). We had electives in art, music, home economics, and even auto mechanics. I excelled in English and science because the teachers were fantastic, and they were exciting, creative, and very engaged in their subjects. Respect was expected, everyone did their homework and discipline was unnecessary. If there was a problem the teacher sent a note home and that was very bad news.

High school graduation in 1952 found me near the top of my class academically and with a scholarship for studies in nursing. I was well on my way to a career, which had been my lifelong dream, and my parents' lifelong dream for all three of their children.

Luckily for Dottie, nursing represented a highly desired line of further study and employment. Yet her account underlines the limited career options put to her, as well as the expectation that as a school girl interested in sport, she would take up cheerleading. In the final chapter of her memoir draft Dottie returns to this theme, but the anecdote seems relevant here:

Growing up with a sports-embracing family certainly had an influence on the children in our family—not just to be a spectator but a participant. I have yet to figure out how my mom could be a high school teacher and yet go to Ladies' Day at the Polo Grounds every week when the Giants played at home. She shared her passion for the Giants games with a neighborhood man who watched the away games on our little black and white TV. We could always tell when he had been at our house because he smoked cigars and the house reeked.

Together these two knew all the batting averages, predicted balls and strikes, who should stay in and who should go, and they also shouted at the "umps" on what they knew were bad calls. Life was never dull with the Giants and not to mention "Them Bums," the Dodgers.

A little aside to the game: on the day Willie Mays came up with the Giants we adopted an orphan cat and it just happened to be black (no racial profiling here because we didn't know what it was). We three kids debated a name for the adoptee and my mom said, "I think we should name him Willie because Willie Mays is going to be one of the greatest players of all time."

So, Willie it was on both counts.

As a child, Dottie hoped to be a nurse. This photograph from the 1930s by her father, Carl Simpson, shows her dressed up as a nurse, posing in front of the family home with her twin brother Richard (Dick) (Dottie Dorion Collection).

Willie became a neighborhood attraction. Whenever the baseball announcer said, "Willie Mays is on deck and coming to bat," the cat would come running from anywhere in the house and jump up on the TV and I know to this day the cat would have been *in the TV* if possible.

I realized how important the sport was to my mom and I thought it was important to me, too. I later played softball and thought of my mom. I also remembered the good meals we had when the Giants won, and the not-so-good meals when they lost.

Beyond Triathlon

My mom would have loved to have the opportunity for sports, and she said, "One day I played volleyball." (And it probably was just one day.) My dad had opportunities in track and football and is recognized in his college Athletic Hall of Fame.

Dottie and her mother may have both enjoyed the benefits of sport, had the opportunity to play seriously presented itself. In part, practical considerations may have constrained Dottie's sporting ambition:

I played tennis and probably could have achieved a ranking, but I always had to work weekends and summers at a variety of jobs: babysitting, department store clerk, and counselor at camps.

But in her various accounts, Dottie acknowledges readily that as she grew up gendered philosophies and expectations framed the culture of sports and the settings in which women and girls were allowed to participate in sport:

In high school and college, we pretty well had dictated training routines with limited knowledge and also limited facilities. I was a competitive participant in all team sports, particularly field hockey, and excelled in gym class.

I realized that boys had more opportunities in gym class. Girls were not supposed to climb ropes, but I could climb ropes very well. Of course, it was a little boring to only be allowed to play a half court in basketball and not have all the sports that were available to boys. Plus, our coaches were leftovers from the boys and were quite insulted to be coaching us in our little maroon bloomer gym suits. A great "real" women's coach in field hockey helped us win a Long Island Championship. We used a bare bones locker room, which on occasion had enough hot water to go around. Forget any vision of a weight room for women, or a Jacuzzi!

I saw it early on and I had that disadvantage all my life. My brother got into track as a pole-vaulter when we were growing up. There was a spare lot next door to where we lived on Long Island, which we made into a little track for him. But there was nothing for me. Sometimes I could pass off as a boy with my twin. We used to go for running events. My father worked for the telephone company and they had events in the summer. I was told "Don't beat the boys," and "There's not too many prizes, so don't take them." You take that with you.

Less interested in and seemingly less talented at sport than Dottie, young Celeste, too, learned quickly the boundaries within which she was permitted to play:

I learned, also, that I was not to act like, God forbid, a tomboy. I was not to climb trees with boys. I was not to play kick ball with them in the

26

street. If such an activity could not be avoided, say, as in school, I was, under no circumstances, to win.

We had physical education in my first year, where we played half court basketball. I seem to remember a stint with volleyball. I hated both and never understood what it was we were supposed to do out there. There were only fifty minutes of gym class, and we had to change clothes, leaving perhaps thirty minutes of playtime. Gym did not change my life.

For three years I went to an American military dependents' high school in Spain and participated in what was called G.A.A., Girls' Athletic Association. We played softball and I was always the last one chosen to be on a team.

I graduated from Catholic High School in 1960 in Columbia, South Carolina, where I was a cheerleader, but so were most girls who were short.

For one year, I went to a Spanish university in Madrid as a junior. There, I played tennis. I was also class president. There was a clay court club not far from our house and I met Charlton Heston there one time. My mother's only admonishment was not to beat any boy I played with. If I did, he would not like me. I had to have boys like me so that one day one would ask me to marry him, so he could take care of me because I could not take care of myself. My mother had allowed me, as she allowed herself to believe, that life was a lark and that letting a man tell you where to set your empties was better than Christmas Day.

Cute and bubble-headed, as well as "good girl," ruled the day.

While Celeste might emphasize discipline, restraint, and dependence, and Dottie might point to the more subtle experience of limited opportunity, both accounts are presented with purpose. Dottie concludes the anecdote about her mother's passion for the Giants with a hint as to where the over-riding narrative of the memoir is heading:

I learned very early—when I couldn't do something—to find a way. My mother gave me the courage to do that because I saw her doing that. She resigned as president of the Garden Club when they wouldn't give membership to an Afro-American.

In both cases, the memoir chapters about childhood point to a problem. In the final sentence of her draft chapter about childhood, Dottie indicates that the memoir is about the ways in which she (and Celeste) dealt with the burden of expectation:

My "baggage" became a reality for the future and an integral part of new growth and adventures.

2

Stage Center

The carefree, energetic twin and the strictly indoctrinated eldest child—one excelling at field hockey, the other at elocution—as Dottie and Celeste tell their stories, their paths do not seem destined to cross.

And yet there is a common thread in their memoir accounts of young adult life. As they write about their journey into adulthood, a picture emerges of young women working toward futures sketched out for them by parents, teachers, and others.

There is also a common silence in their accounts about this phase in their lives. Celeste places emphasis on some parts of her story and over-looks others. She says little about moments that might have been antici-pated eagerly and cherished highly at the time. The aim of the memoir is clearly not to provide fodder for a romantic comedy (set in the Mid-West in the 1960s for its own twist on a conventional filmic genre).

After one year as a junior at the University of Madrid, I gradu-ated from the Jesuit Creighton University in Omaha where I was on the Dean's List. I got no awards to speak of other than the award for top English student and I think the top Spanish award in the University.

One incident crept back into my mind about four decades after it happened, which, at the time, was not an incident at all. *The Three Faces of Eve* had been showing at the local Bijou.

"I think I'd like to be a psychiatrist," I told my dad one day.

"You can't," he said.

"Why?"

"Because it's too hard."

"Oh," I replied, turning back to the book I was reading and appre-ciating yet another clue as to how my life should be led. Don't try hard stuff.

Now I understand that he meant to say that he had four sons to edu-cate and that I would marry and not need such an expensive education. I was to go to a good school to meet an eligible man. And that's a quote.

2. Stage Center

So I graduated from a Jesuit university with majors in English and Spanish and minors in education and philosophy and became a high school English and Spanish teacher, which I loved. But it was "something to fall back on." Even though I wrote my husband's papers for his MBA and later became a three-time champion on *Jeopardy*, I never got to use anything I ever learned about Aristotle and Aquinas.

One year turned into the next. Doing what I was told to do, I lived out the hopes of others. My parents were high-minded, and my guardian angel sits on the bench for the Rams, so as I approached adulthood, I was in good field position to grab the prize that was the purpose of my life.

A good husband.

In the early '60s, there was no serial monogamy. We dated different guys almost every night. It was fun, but I knew it was only a prelude. Soon would begin the Husband Hunt. I loved teaching but after two years, I started to choose among my suitors, if I may. Richard John Callahan, a popular football star who had graduated from the University of Nebraska, won the draw. My parents had sent me to Creighton—said Jesuit school—and not to the University of Nebraska. I think that's funny, but no one really laughs.

We married in Omaha October 19, 1968, and had three children, almost right away: Kelly, Tim and Colin. Dick joined Bell Systems, the local telephone company. He began to move up the ladder and across the globe just the way my father had, ending up in London as head of U.S. West International. When Bell decided that cellular was never going to be big, Dick got out and started his own company in London. He was on the ground floor of the revolution in communication technology.

As with my father, we moved every two to three years. We lived all over—Iowa, New Jersey (while Dick worked in New York City), Minnesota, South Dakota, Washington State, and then Denver, Colorado. Taught well, I could move house on the same dime on which my mother had moved hers. I liked that I could stay home and did not have to put on pantyhose to leave the house at dawn. All I had to do was live my life for others.

And I did.

Marriage and children followed shortly after graduation for Dottie as well. In contrast to Celeste, she continued to work in her chosen profession of nursing, in part out of necessity. Dottie might appear to present a more comprehensive and less cynical narrative. Yet she, too, compresses the journey from daughter to wife and mother into a handful of paragraphs that center more on the paid and unpaid work performed during those years, than anything else:

I met George Dorion on a blind date after he saw a photo of me and liked my legs! He was an impressive guy and very funny. He had served three years in the Air Force and was doing graduate work at Yale. On our first date we had dinner with his parents. How did that all work out? We married in 1957, after I graduated with honors from Columbia University Nursing School. We have just celebrated our sixty-third anniversary.

In the early years of marriage, one is so busy and working so hard that you don't think too much of the future. Just making it day to day is the name of the game. My husband was running chemical experiments at Yale University Chemical Laboratory and working odd hours depending on his "burning and baking" schedule. Much of the time we were like "ships passing in the night." He also studied for oral exams, which were essential to pass in order to graduate with his doctoral degree.

I was teaching nursing at Grace New Haven Hospital to help support him. Nursing today is a different world, with a lot more aid from technology. It was the dark age, with twenty to thirty patients each and no help. My nurse's uniform was still the Columbia blue and white stripes, apron, bib, starched cap, proud graduate pin, and name tag. Quite a change from today's nondescript scrubs, which require a game of hide and seek to find the nurse's name tag. No point looking for a nurse's cap. The latter, in many different styles, once proudly identified the school of nursing from which you graduated. I loved nursing though and am still very involved.

I was teaching on all shift schedules: days, relief and nights. Fortunately, I took our old car to work. I was as young looking as the students and got quite used to having someone ask, "Where is your instructor?" And there I was, standing right there. It was demanding to cover the whole hospital and I scooted around in an electric cart in the basement. It was stressful and my day never ended until every student had finished giving meds (since I was teaching pharmacology). There was no room for error and my rule was, "You are right 100% of the time or you fail and are OUT!"

While few career options were presented to Dottie, nursing was not something that she chose grudgingly. After my visit to her home in Florida, she wrote more about the pride she felt about her work in the nursing profession:

Can I ever describe what it means to be a NURSE?

The nurses of yesteryear were prepared to give meds, make beds,

George Dorion proposed to Dottie in 1957 on the same day that she graduated from the Columbia University School of Nursing (Dottie Dorion Collection).

handle emergencies, boil/sterilize equipment, perform wound care, and empty bedpans. We even whipped up a poultice or two (What's that?). All patients had handwritten notes about their condition. We served wards with many patients and it's hard to believe that at night each patient under our care had a backrub before sleep.

Making beds was not an easy task. Mattresses had to be turned, plastic covering on top, sheets (not fitted) had to be tucked tightly, top sheet had to have exactly six inches on top turndown, square corners were perfect, and a spread was even hung all the way around.

This was the world of the '50s, and it gave us great pride in our work, our professionalism, our devotion to our patients. Today, the modern age of nursing, things are very different. The world of technology runs the hospitals and nurses. One day I was visiting a patient in a hospital and there was a power outage. Everyone stood around in helpless mode and unable to function. I made a few suggestions, which definitely "Fell on Deaf Ears."

Nursing had to change, education had to change, and the entire medical community had to change. Nursing schools had to change with the times or be gone. They had to update teaching skills and incorporate computer driven patient care. They had to establish Simulation Labs where nurses could practice every procedure with computer feedback. Years later, I was involved in introducing Simulation Labs at University of North Florida. Today I serve on the Board, Committees and endow scholarships at The Columbia University School of Nursing, formerly The Columbia Presbyterian Medical Center. The new seven-story, state of the art Nursing School, attests to the great vision and leadership of The School. Yes, indeed "The Times They Are a Changin."

In my lifetime of nursing I was able to work in thirteen different jobs all over the country and all with great satisfaction. I am so proud that our generation was "The Pioneer in Nursing," and those before us, and those before them.

Using the past to explain the present in this sketch of the evolving occupation of nursing, Dottie does not deny the strengths of earlier generations of nurses and the tradition into which she gained access. Here and elsewhere she implies that the profession in the present—while transformed significantly—draws on the rigor, the experience, and the lessons drawn by the nurses of her time and those before them. Change, in Dottie's teleology, does not appear to represent a rupture from the past, but rather rests on the past. It is possible to both respect and improve on tradition.

2. Stage Center

As it was, Dottie's nursing career meant that she could contribute constructively to the household income, as her memoir recounts:

Our income was extremely limited, and the G.I. Bill helped greatly, a result of my husband's service in the U.S. Air Force. We were so happy that we had a "real" apartment and didn't have to live in the Quonset huts [*prefabricated structures with curved galvanized steel sides and ceiling*] that were available—many of our friends had no choice. When times were financially tough, we had potluck suppers and usually it was our ordinary staples but we gathered together, shared and had fun aside from work. The Lab supplied alcohol for punch because we were too poor to afford much else! Sometimes worried parents who thought we were surely starving to death would send CARE packages—usually the canned goods were nowhere near our needed staples, but it was the thought that counted.

We worked really hard. George finished his Ph.D. early and went to work in Stamford, Connecticut. When we had saved enough money, we took several months off and toured Europe on $5.00 a day! It was the chance of a lifetime because we never had that much free time again. We were happy to meet his parents in England after several weeks. We went to their "real" hotel for afternoon tea and the luxury began: the tea trolley, loaded with tiers of rich food, rolled toward us and when they asked, "Would you like something?" We replied, "Yes, please, one of everything."

After the trip we started raising a family. We started our brood in New Canaan, Connecticut, in 1959. Soon we had four children, three boys and one girl: Mark, Christopher, Timothy and Lisanne.

Everyone knows that with children to raise you just keep going one day at a time. The cloth diapers were soaked in every bathroom toilet and then put into a hamper for the diaper service to pick up. The smell was sometimes overwhelming, and NO disinfectant could erase that penetrating odor. Big diaper safety pins became dull over time and the pinholes in our fingers became a badge of honor.

School, activities, carpools, hand-me-down clothes, sickness, short two week vacations to visit grandparents or special U.S. parks, and the kids just kept growing: outgrowing shoes, skates and skis. There was no day care, mostly high school age babysitters, a cleaning lady half a day every two weeks, an old station wagon (this is before seat belts), wrestling matches in the back, black and white T.V. and dressing and undressing kids in the winter took most of the day. We did almost everything with other families and didn't miss anything else because we were all in it together and didn't know otherwise!

Beyond Triathlon

I was still working as an instructor trainee at Red Cross on weekends and at night and dragged the children with me. I also started a Master of Special Education at New Haven College in Connecticut in 1959. I spent the years in between each child finishing the Master's degree. When I graduated ten years later the College was much bigger, becoming eventually the Southern Connecticut University.

After I graduated with Master's in 1969, we moved from Connecticut, to California, to Puerto Rico and to Florida. My husband worked for an environmental company, then in waste management. When we got back to Florida in 1971, he helped build a laboratory for quality control and other buildings followed.

By the time we moved to Florida, the children were moving into high school. We found a school near Deerwood where we lived, the Jacksonville Episcopal High School. Soon they were off to colleges and beyond.

Neither Dottie nor Celeste tell stories that celebrate motherhood or social mobility. By the early 1970s, both women had everything—successful husbands, material comforts, healthy children, their own qualifications and interests, and active social lives. Yet their accounts suggest that just as the imagined futures became realities—when it might seem they had full, satisfying lives—something was missing. This is most evident when Dottie and Celeste attempt to write not about work or family, but about their sporting lives, in particular, about playing tennis.

In Dottie's memoir, her paragraph on tennis is typically modest and brief. Reading it left me intrigued. In response to my questions, she wrote a little more. She offers more clues, more details. Her sketch of social tennis now has a little more shading, more depth and more highlights. I wonder whether, by sharing it, I might alter Dottie's original design. But, as with the memoir, the sketch is designed to draw the eye toward something she wants her reader to see. Even when Dottie elaborates on her tennis background, it is still interwoven with the familiar contextual narrative of marriage, professional development and the struggle for economic stability and advancement:

How I would have loved to have the opportunity after college to have more than two choices for sport: golf or tennis.

Since I was already playing tennis in my younger years and later at the School of Nursing [S.O.N.], that was my choice. On vacations at home, I played a little golf, mostly to please my parents. However, I felt that little white demon on the tee was out to get me and I hated the chase to beat it.

2. Stage Center

While at the S.O.N., there were tennis courts in the beautiful gardens in back of the main medical center. I chose an elective at The Eye Institute, feeling guilty now, so I could play tennis nearby and then go to work. It was quite a challenge. I could change into a complete uniform going up in the elevator and this included: starched long sleeved blue and white striped uniform buttoned from wrist to neck and skirt hanging to the floor. Many buttons were a challenge. Then the starched apron and bib with name pin on, more buttons. And, alas, then the freshly ironed cap (cost $0.25 to have it ironed) with bobby pins attached. Of course, black shoes to complete our professional ensemble. Only graduates wore white shoes and stockings. Some days I was a little breathless but with a little deodorant, less odorous from smelly sweat.

I actually loved working there, besides the proximity to tennis courts. It was totally quiet to let patients rest without any loud noises to disturb them. It was here I saw miracles every day. When blind patients had surgery and when they removed their bandages, for the first time they could SEE! All the staff could then break the silence rule and celebrate.

When I graduated, became engaged, and planned a marriage it took "stage center." I worked as a camp nurse and I remember writing our wedding invitations in the camp dining room, crouched under a table with a sheet covering our writing duties to keep mosquitoes out. Many an invite was engraved with protein.

As newlyweds my husband finished his Ph.D. thesis, we traveled Europe, and rented eventually a small "cottage" in Connecticut. Finally, I could return to sports. We joined the New Canaan Field Club and both of us played tennis. Also, we had excellent public courts nearby.

In winter I skied and played platform tennis. Platform tennis was only a big sport in some places because there were not many platform tennis courts. You played on half sized, fenced tennis courts, and could play the ball off the fences.

I played tennis as often as I could with a growing family of four young children—remember, cloth diapers, no daycare or babysitters. I had some lovely partners for women's doubles, and we won many tournaments. We were accused of winning only because one or the other of us was pregnant. Our opponents were scared that we were going to deliver on the court. Or, we had so many interruptions to breast feed a baby or chase the children that we won by distraction.

Working in Southern California ten years later, I had finished graduate school and played level "B" and level "A" tennis tournaments around that area. It was very competitive. Later moving to Puerto Rico, I played tournaments there at various clubs. At one finals at a hotel there, early in the morning, I slipped on a sandy court and dislocated my knee. This necessitated a straight leg plaster cast for three months. I said goodbye to tennis for a while. We had to make several airplane trips for family events off the island. It was a rude awakening to travel with this disability, especially when using the bathroom. My husband stood guard outside the open door, since it couldn't shut with my cast sticking out.

We returned to Jacksonville, Florida, in 1971, to bring the company business here and start building and operations. We chose to live in a new residential club area, kind of, "Out in the Woods." It was a little like "The Wild West." Alligators in our backyard, boar pigs roaming around, deer on the roads, snakes in our garage etc.

I planned to play tennis at the club and tennis courts nearby. When I called to offer to play on a team I was turned down. "No idea why." Shortly afterwards, I went over to the courts to introduce myself in person and maybe even play. I met a team captain and she was more than shocked to see me, very surprised. She thought I was Black because I had come from Puerto Rico.

Anecdotally Dottie affirms that tennis at Jacksonville was a little different to her previous experiences:

I was finally accepted on the Deerwood Golf and Country Club tennis team—the local neighborhood team—when they realized I wasn't black. The women's tennis team was quite different from what I had been accustomed to in previous locations. I played for many years on the "A" team and participated in challenge matches to determine my position in the ranking. I played all over California. But I had to play one match, then another, and travel. I didn't want to neglect family. Here—at Deerwood—there were A, B and C teams.

There was a downside to neighborhood tennis, as Dottie describes in her memoir:

Most of the players didn't want to play singles for fear of losing. Most were friendly and made doubles enjoyable. But there were others who wanted to win at any cost, even miscalling lines and hitting balls at your face.

As the neighborhood grew and more competitors joined the teams it became something of an all day affair with pep rallies, partners wearing matching outfits like the Bobbsey Twins [*central characters in a long running series of children's novels*], car decorations for away matches, and lunches after the matches. It was cheerleading sort of stuff.

2. Stage Center

The year I was team captain was the beginning of the end. When husbands started calling me with threats—"How dare you make my wife play with so and so"—and challenge matches necessitated 6 a.m. telephone calls....

Enough!

Celeste's background in tennis was minimal, casual at best, but she soon found herself striving to do more than simply propel a ball over the net. As she tells it, her adult experience of tennis was driven by a need to play well, to win:

My husband had a profound influence on my sporting life, albeit inadvertent.

Critical moment: one afternoon, in our early marriage, when my husband came home from a new job in a new state.

"What did you get done?" he asked, ever the list maker.

"I joined the Newcomers. And I played *tennis!*"

In telling this story Celeste omits such details as the state into which she had moved or the tennis courts where she played. Later, she elaborated:

This was in New Jersey. The tennis courts were in a public park and you had to sign up at a police station.

She also omits to explain in her memoir that tennis did not represent her only attempt to fill her days with something interesting as a young wife settling into a new home in New Jersey. I discovered subsequently that she enjoyed some notoriety as a champion on the popular television game show Jeopardy *during this period. But such details are tangential to Celeste's original point, which centers on the reaction of her husband, Dick, to the revelation that she played tennis:*

"Did you win?"

I let that one register for about two beats. Here was new information. "I don't remember."

And then the zapper: "it's much more fun when you win."

So what followed, then, was years—almost a decade—of playing in the A leagues.

In a document written separately when I asked why she struggled with tennis, Celeste explained the national ranking system:

If you were a 4 or 4.5 player, you were an A; 3 or 3.5 was a B player.

I played singles and doubles in two tennis clubs in two sequential states. We moved from New Jersey to Minnesota—there was a very competitive club there—and then to South Dakota where we played at the Westward Ho Country Club. I got to be competitive; I got to be OK with it.

Dick and I played doubles and did very well, but a lot of yelling ensued—"That was yours!"

One day we won the over thirty-five category at the state championships. I would win my serve because the person on the opposing team was standing too far back and I could return everything. We had a break and I went home to start lasagna: a woman's story—having people for dinner. As I took the lasagna out, I poured boiling water on my stomach and hand. I was in the bathroom putting cold water on it when my husband called out, "Are you coming?"

I told him about the burn.

"Which hand?"

So we were good together except for the fighting part.

And it was important to win. When I didn't win, I would lay on the couch upset with myself, while the kids napped.

That is part of the journey. The women were not the competitors. There was none of this "I'll kill you with this shot," and then go and have a beer like men. It was like who you were as a person. You took it with you.

Celeste provides none of these details in her memoir, but she makes it clear that her experiences with tennis proved unsatisfying:

Actually I hated tennis. I hated large groups of women who played tennis. I hated large groups of women who, after playing tennis, went to lunch and talked about adding cream of mushroom soup to anything that went on the table. I hated that I felt that my sum worth depended on whether I won or lost a tennis match on any particular morning: in my eyes, in the eyes of the women, and in what I imagined would be those of my husband as well. Not "as well." Most of all. I required the praise from my husband that I did not get from my dad. My report card was made out by the chief men in my life.

Why did Dottie and Celeste struggle with tennis? As presented in their memoirs, something about the culture of neighborhood tennis appears to trouble them. Both women seem uncomfortable also with the wish to be competitive. For Celeste it seems to tie into a need for external forms of validation; while Dottie's accounts suggest that she prioritized family responsibilities over any desire to realize her full sporting potential.

Are either of these points significant in themselves? Why do Dottie and Celeste emphasize social tennis in their memoirs? Reflecting on what they include and what they leave out of the memoir accounts about this phase in their lives, I realize that the point may not actually be about tennis. Perhaps tennis is just a clue—pink tape tied to a tree along the narrative trail—to tell their readers where they are going. I might be curious about the culture of social tennis, but like the tales they tell about marriage and maternity, tennis does not take center stage in the memoirs. Their answers lie somewhere further along the trail.

3

In the Middle of an
Ivory Soap Commercial

Conventional narratives, whether in book or film, introduce the central characters and set up a "problem" that—once it becomes apparent—disrupts any appearance of normality, creates the drama, and drives the over-riding storyline. Mounting grievances with tennis might appear to provide the disruptive energy that leads to a sequence of new directions in the respective life stories told by Dottie and Celeste and to resolution. But from my reading of their memoirs, I would suggest that social tennis was not the problem so much as a sign. On their respective narrative trails social tennis is just a foothill, a sign that we are approaching a mountain range.

The accounts provided by Dottie and Celeste regarding what came next are enormously entertaining, as might be expected, when oft-rehearsed anecdotes of trial and error, and moments of self-fulfillment, are told decades later.

Dottie was the first to give up on tennis, quitting dramatically in the first half of the 1970s. It was only a year or two after the family moved to Jacksonville:

I quit "cold turkey."

When I informed my family of the decision to quit tennis, they all looked rather horrified.

"What are you going to do now with all your energy, you'll drive us nuts?"

That's true.

Enter our eldest son who was running track in high school and generously offered to take me out running in our neighborhood. I put on my tennis sneakers, shorts and a tee shirt and joined our son to run half a mile around the lake where we lived.

Well, it was one big rude awakening. I could not run without stopping every few hundred yards. I was huffing and puffing and thought my heart would jump out of my chest or else I was about to have a heart attack. I remember being really angry because I was so bad and had no cardio conditioning from ladies tennis doubles. Doubles tennis is not so good for cardio conditioning. Single is much better. And of course, our son, now a world-class ultramarathoner, was keeping a fast pace.

I vowed from that day that I would one day run a marathon.

At first, I called myself a "closet" runner. In the beginning, I ran at night so no one would see me. When I started running, I thought, "Oh, anybody can run!" But changed my mind straight away—it was really hard! I was kind of embarrassed because I didn't know if I was running right.

Also, I weighed a bit more and had a few jiggly bits. I had flab in all the wrong places, so I was very self-conscious. And I didn't know what you should really wear. I don't remember there being any running clothes or anything.

Nor were there any running shoes in my size. The only shoes available were for men. At first I ran in tennis sneakers, but our son had some running shoes. I remember trying to run in them with insoles.

But running is a single sport for you and you only. Trying to improve and get better keeps you going.

Celeste also took up running in the 1970s. Unlike Dottie, Celeste did not do so as a result of a direct rejection of tennis. And her family was younger. Like Dottie, Celeste grew impatient with social tennis just a year or two after moving home and deepening restlessness drove her to embrace an activity that held no initial appeal:

Once I was sitting on a black and yellow hide-a-bed couch, watching *Edge of Night* [television show] and folding diapers. Suddenly I realized that I did not know how I had gotten there.

We had three small children; I lived in a nice house. But in the middle of an Ivory Soap commercial, I realized that the life I was living was not my own.

That night in bed I told my husband that I felt like running away. Because he only listens to part of what I say, he replied, turning to his other side: "Just make sure you get some good running shoes first."

We were in Minnesota when that happened. My youngest son was born in 1976 and we moved to Sioux Falls, South Dakota, when Colin was a year old.

One day, sometime after relocating our family home—yet again— my husband asked me to *run* to the tennis courts, about two blocks away. I could not.

That scared me.

A few weeks later, the doorbell rang just after supper. This, in Sioux Falls. Two friends had run over, as in *run*, from Pendar Lane about half a mile away. I was gob smacked. The next day I measured by car the rectangular park that contained the aforementioned tennis courts. Eight tenths of a mile. So when the seven year old came home from school to watch the five and one year olds—I'd be arrested today for same—I left by the back door to walk-run around the park.

Learning to run the eight tenths of a mile without stopping was the longest two weeks of my entire life. I *loathed* it. I would run full out—*jogging* had not yet been invented—the two shorter sides of the park. And I would run-walk the long sides, making myself, each day, run a few steps further and walk a few steps fewer than the day before. I'd keep my eyes fixed onto that blue mailbox on the corner of 18th as though it signaled the Promised Land.

My major issue with running was that there was nothing to do *while* doing it. Had I been able to scotch tape a book to my sunglasses, I would have felt the endeavor time worthy. As it was, here we had about fifteen minutes of nothing, of time wasted. But I was determined to be able to do what I could not, especially since two friends had run a half mile to my house as though—as though what? I hate the overuse of the word *surreal*. But that's what it was.

Having equivocated about the use of the term "surreal," Celeste's decision to go with the word is instructive: it suggests that to her, at that point in time, the idea of running somewhere, anywhere, for the sake of running seemed unbelievable. Possibly it was more than that. Perhaps the idea of running as an activity seemed like something that might happen in an alternate reality, in another life. Not the life that she has been describing.

So, one foot in front of the other, one day following the next, I kept at it. I cannot describe the pride I felt the day I ran the whole thing. I just looked up the word "accomplishment," but it falls flat describing what I had not felt, ever, in my life before. A nun's cheating the system by helping me, the face of an angel, through a physics test: that was just the execution of one of my coping skills. Running around McKennan Park in the spring of 1978 was the result of endurance, concentration, determination, and hard work—concepts heretofore unknown to me. I have not considered this moment of abject satisfaction ever before. But maybe it was *that one* that changed my life and the lives of the women I would go on, decades later, to help also to change.

Two ideas.

3. In the Middle of an Ivory Soap Commercial

One, I felt so much better after my 3:00 p.m. ten-minute run. For the first time, I was alone. I had time to myself. I had not been alone for many years. After that hot shower and redressing for supper, I felt … new. I no longer had winter cabin fever. I had … energy. I had put on my own oxygen mask and now could help others with theirs.

Two, the idea that if I worked hard for something—even if, and especially if, that something were outside both my ken and comfort zone—I could actually reach it, was new to me. Sure. I had always worked hard. Making the Dean's List in university and cleaning the house and keeping toddlers from hanging themselves was not the stuff of sloths. But those things were within the boundaries of my life as that life had been designed for me.

I've always thought that, when you are born, you stand at, say, a golf clubhouse door, and someone hands you a set of clubs: they may be state of the art, they may be from Toys R Us, but these are your tools for what you are about to do. You are also given a course on which to play. My tools were good. My course was easy.

What I was about to do was change golf courses—with the clubs I had.

Or. To mix metaphors: I stood prepared to push back the boundaries within which I had lived. Until then, I had no idea that they had confined me. But, then, I guess, that's what boundaries do.

Celeste has more to say about this particular benefit of running later in her memoir, but both Dottie and Celeste also identify other more immediate and direct benefits of running. As Dottie noted, there was one obvious one:

When I started running, I wasn't really in shape. I thought I was in shape but really wasn't. I weighed at least ten pounds more than now. I started losing weight and gained more muscle definition in the calves and so on. It makes a difference. I realized running was a tremendous asset for good health. And I could wear better clothing! Of course, you like to look good. I was young. Who doesn't want to look good?

For Celeste, the benefit was also social. It gave her something—and somebody—outside of the ordinary obligations associated with family and home.

What I did first was to turn that eight tenths of a mile into one. Then two. And then three. And then I called Jan, one of the women who had appeared at my front door that night, and asked if she would like to go for a run. Jan had four small children, the oldest younger than my second child. Indeed, she would like to go for a run.

So once a week, after school, we would hire proper sitters and run three miles.

I had a friend.

In my day, we did not have female friends. We had props: girls to go with you to the bathroom at a party, girls to talk to when the boys would not. Girlfriends were treated as suspects. They would turn on you on that same turning dime. The boys were the goal. Girlfriends were stepping stones or stopping blocks towards the guys. There was never a level of trust with girlfriends in the fifties or the sixties. Girls, and then women, represented variants of "be a threat to me and I will kill you." Nope, we did not have girlfriends.

But Jan and I became friends. How? Friendship, I finally figured, requires vulnerability. Two women with the same golf clubs heading out on a course that has been designed to make them look foolish. Jan would say that the run seemed hard that day, and I would address her message, not rate the messenger. "For me, too." I might have answered. She felt heard. And so she might offer something else—a problem with the husband. Or an untold insecurity. We had to pass the time. And as I am loud and she is not, I found that, to *be* a friend, I had to listen. If she questioned the pace, I would hear her out and acquiesce. But I had to listen very well and listen between her euphemisms and habit of good cheer. So as she became a friend by offering herself, I learned to become one also.

Me and my friend just ran. My friend and I.

In contrast to Celeste, Dottie ran initially with her husband and son and hid her new hobby from other women:

One day a friend made a comment to me, "You know I saw someone running down our Boulevard and it looked just like you!" "Oh, no, that couldn't have been me." You can guess. I just changed the subject.

But necessity forced Dottie to demonstrate publicly her growing capacity for distance running:

My early running career took many interesting turns.... In the mid–1970s I worked as a consultant on a Diagnostic and Evaluation Team, which placed school children with learning disabilities in special programs. At one time I directed a summer day camp. One day my proficiency in running came in very handy. A camper, Patrick, took off and started running. He headed off school property toward the swamp with alligators. I took off in fast pursuit, sweating profusely in the hundred-degree heat.

"Had I met my match?" I wondered.

As I got closer to the swamp the stench was overwhelming.

"Just keep going...."

We both ended up in the swamp where alligators were lying in wait. We quickly exited and I told Patrick, "I will never give up on you but if you ever do that again you'll have Holy Hell to pay."

I still keep in touch with him to this day.

In the 1970s sufficient numbers of women embraced distance running for some magazines and sports brands to begin to see them as a promising new market. But Dottie and Celeste both learned to run with limited access to guides, products and common interest groups. Celeste had Jan and Dottie had George, but the transition to runner was a solitary journey, mostly. And conducted with limited knowledge about the science behind the activity, as Celeste recounts:

We just ran. We ran without water. We ran without watches. We did not know that we were on the edge of a trend that would take over the world. We did not know there were rules or regulations or training tips.

Dottie benefited from the accumulated knowledge of her husband, George, who ran at college and her son, Mark, who ran track at school. Yet she, too, felt quite isolated as a woman learning to run. She was not part of a team, had no coach, and many of the key books for runners came out a few years after her first tentative efforts to circumnavigate the lake at Deerwood.

It was really hard running in the early years when women weren't running. They were primarily playing tennis or golf in our era. My husband was traveling a lot. If I was brave and ran in daylight, I might occasionally find a neighborhood man jogging around and join him. But one wife got upset. One day she drove by, saw me running with her husband and ran *me* off the road!

With running I didn't think about being competitive, just trying to improve. And the good thing when you start any sport at a low level, you see yourself improving. I was really just concentrating on trying to go a bit faster and run longer. I saw other people about my age and thought, "They're running faster than me." I would think, "Why can't I run faster?" My husband advised that I should build up gradually and do a bit of speed work. I found out from my son that I should do track.

There were a couple of books out: Joan Ullyot—that was the first book I remember—and George Sheehan's *Medical advice for runners.* But there wasn't a whole lot.

Joan Ullyot's first book was published in 1976 and Sheehan's in 1978. When she started, Dottie had nothing serious to consult for guidance.

Nor were there many fun runs, or women competing in fun runs, particularly in Jacksonville when Dottie first started running. Prior to the foundation of what was then known as the Jacksonville Track Club in 1975, the only regular fun run in the area was the Summer Beach Run. With the club's arrival came the Winter Beach Run and a few fun runs out of Florida Junior College. These provided opportunities that Dottie embraced, though somewhat self-consciously.

In Jacksonville they had a fun run for kids. They were just a couple of miles—very low key—and run out of the junior college here. At first, I finished last, with little kids going by. I was embarrassed. Later I was excited because I wasn't last. I wanted to be competitive but didn't know what I was doing.

For both Dottie and Celeste, their first major running events proved pivotal. As Dottie recounts, her first major event was the inaugural ten-kilometer Bonne Bell Mini Marathon in 1977:

Despite feeling self-conscious and slow when she first started running in the early 1970s, Dottie quickly improved and became an active member of the Jacksonville Track Club (courtesy George Dorion).

My first BIG race was The Bonne Bell in Boston, a 10K race held in the 1970s. I was very apprehensive. It was such a big deal.

When I picked up the race pack I was really impressed, thinking, "Wow, is this what it's all about?" And, "If this is what it's all about, I'm in." It had all these gifty things: a tee shirt, and a "goodie bag" with neat stuff.

It was a cool drizzly morning. At the start they had music and we huddled together. I was mushed in with all these women and we were all shivering from nerves or cold or both. I was so excited to be with these hundreds of women, who were all doing the same thing.

I had not even a clue if I could finish, but I planned nine-minute miles. I started to get tired around the four-mile mark and I came to some stairs to cross over the river and it looked scary. My husband was there, encouraging me on.

Then, I saw two volunteers carrying a woman in a wheelchair up the stairs and I knew, I really knew, that to finish is golden. I would finish. When I passed that FINISH banner and heard the announcer say my name and where I was from, I said to myself, "Look out world ... here I come."

I was thrilled to have one success. And to find out you're not alone, not the odd person out. Not knowing if you're doing anything right and then seeing that you can be competitive, be in the group and not last, was such a great feeling.

Bonne Bell was fantastic.

Celeste and Jan had barely mastered running three miles continuously when Dick encouraged Celeste to participate in her first fun run:

Then one day, something else happened. Dick asked if Jan and I would run in a 5K he was organizing for the Howard Wood Dakota Relays, a spring sports meet at which, in high school, he had starred.

Sure, we said. We had no idea what a 5K was. We found that it is a citizen's running race that includes a lot of people of both genders, starting together, all bunched up and running until there appears a finish line. The distance is 3.1 miles.

We signed up.

The first Big Positive Surprise was that we got a tee shirt that said 5K on it. I was going to get to wear a tee shirt that touted an athletic event that included boys!

I have a picture of us at the start line. We stood *on* the start line and were surprised that so many people would dare to run past us as the gun went off. Sometime mid-event, we passed about four of our male friends—that is, husbands of our women "friends."

That night at a dinner party, what happened was Big Positive Surprise Number Two. Dick and I walked in the front door of the home of the dinner party givers. As was the way back then, the women were in the kitchen, and the men were in the front room around the television set. But as we wiped our feet, the male faces turned towards us. Toward me: "Celeste! How was the run?" A *man* was speaking to me ... about *me*. About something I had done that did not involve children or was not the immediate result of my husband's stunning deeds. He saw me as me. It gave me some recognition. You who got your formal education after Title IX or 1978 have no idea of the import of this moment.

Dick at the breakfast table: "I never ... thought ... I would be married ... to a woman ... who would get up ... early on a Sunday morning ... to look for her name in the sports section of the newspaper."

Clearly Dottie and Celeste place considerable weight on their transformation into runners, and their accounts are instructive. Both seemed to contrast solitary experiences with collective experiences, being alone to being part of something. Yet the measure of inclusion, the basis of personal satisfaction is expressed in very different terms—Celeste relished recognition by men, Dottie strove for and savored proof of her capacity as an athlete.

The narrative trails have not yet converged, but the stories Dottie and Celeste tell have something in common—they are not trite fairy-tales of empowerment. Their stories reveal that many factors contribute to and impede feelings of enhanced freedom, confidence and empowerment. They show that not all sporting experiences are transformative, but that running did represent a rupture of sorts for both Dottie and Celeste. While their narrative paths do not intersect yet, both appear to point their readers to the same landmark, a rocky outcrop that cracks the horizon in two. For some reason running made a difference, where tennis did not.

4

The Odd Person Out

For both Dottie and Celeste, their first major running events represented simply a beginning. Many more running events—further afield and longer—followed.

Celeste and Jan chased more race memorabilia—they ran for the medals and trophies, and especially for the race tee shirts, as Celeste explains:

Awards were given usually for men and then women, in two age categories: under thirty-five, and thirty-five and over. We usually came in first and second, changing order from time to time without caring which of us came first. We usually crossed the finish line together. In late summer, I turned thirty-five years old. So between us, we would win in both categories.

We liked the hardware. But most of all we loved the tee shirts. The tee shirt was the impetus. We wanted more. So we signed up for every 5K—some of them even four mile—events, that came our way.

Dottie says less about why she participated in more running events, but she clearly gained something that was rewarding personally from the Bonne Bell Mini Marathon. Nor does she comment specifically about the race tee shirts. Yet, among the surprising volume of memorabilia squashed into a storage shop worth of plastic tubs in her Jacksonville home are myriad tee shirts from running events held in the late 1970s and early 1980s. Often devoid of useful dates and details, a comparison of the treasured items of clothing to event histories reveals that Dottie competed in numerous inaugural running events, particularly in Florida.

By the start of 1978, Dottie and George were involved in the Jacksonville Track Club, and active contributors to the expansion of its raft of events:

Around 1978 I got the track club to hold an all-women's race, which went well. That was around the same time as the first River Run. The track club was small then, and to even think of holding a 15K race in

Jacksonville in 1978 was kind of a pipe dream. When "the Father" of River Run, Buck Fannin, came to some of his track club friends to ask their opinions on this proposal it was mostly negative responses. And rightly so, since this proposed course went over two huge bridges, over actively used railroad tracks, and through upscale neighborhoods that would surely protest.

Being a very wise man, and a lawyer too, he persisted with the city and notables who could help clear the obstacles, and there were many. However, the race did get organized and took place with a minimum of fuss. Yes, the railroad gates had to close for a train; many of the finish cards being handed out blew away; and the backup at the Finish Line looked like Macys on sale day.

Notables of That Day: The race director had prize money in a brown paper bag, which was left on the hood of his moving car (remember we could only pay under the table in those days) but later recovered; work crews stayed up all night preparing the course and painting direction arrows by hand; and music on course included a calliope and bands.

We offered to have a big party afterwards with a big tent, band and buffet. The post-race party at our home for all the V.I.P. invited runners continued to be an annual event for years and is still remembered by the elites.

Now the River Run is a huge event, and very professionally done. It's come a long way.

Dottie participated regularly in the River Run, secured more than her fair share of age group trophies for podium finishes, and built a sizable collection of newspaper reports noting her successes.

But she did not run alone: Dottie enjoyed sharing her new found abilities with her children and husband George. Just two months after Bonne Bell and a few months before the inaugural River Run, the pair decided to enter a "mini marathon." It was the first Florida Citrus Bowl Half Marathon Road Race, then known more simply as the Tangerine Bowl Road Race:

It was exciting that my husband and I were both running together; one always had companionship for fun runs and races. Otherwise a woman felt like "The odd person out" since there were so few females out there.

To show how ignorant we were about running, we went to Orlando to run a "mini-marathon," which to us was a 10K. Didn't take long before we realized it was not a manageable 10K, but indeed a Half Marathon. Yikes!

Dottie participated as part of "Team Dorion" with her sons Chris (left) and Tim (right) at a marathon in 1984 (courtesy George Dorion).

It was a most unpleasant race. Not only were there few spectators, it kept going and going. It went by the water and there was this great big boat fixing area where they were painting or spraying boats. The fumes were asphyxiating. For blocks I thought I was going to be sick. It was really bad. It was a nightmare.

Every mile was agony especially when spectators said, "Finish just up ahead, just around the corner," etc. The encouragement would shoot our endorphins up to keep going only to find that "the Yellow Brick Road" just kept going and going. I really couldn't pace myself and alternated between walking and jogging. Finally we crossed over the railroad tracks and we were there. We were not trained for that distance. We had no idea.

We didn't really know much about nutrition, either. All I knew was "have a bit of toast and something to drink." But I was also told, "don't eat or drink too much because you'll be sick." I don't think I knew anything about carbo-loading. As races got bigger, they had pasta parties beforehand. Otherwise we didn't know much. We were pretty ignorant.

But sometimes—when the situation is not so good—you can laugh about it later. George and I were comparing our stories of the "mini marathon" and we both said the fumes were the worst. Sometimes you remember different things. Different races are fun, and you pick out certain things you remember, but more often you remember something that was bad, rather than really good. That's what I remember about Orlando. I was really dying.

The half marathon at Orlando may have registered in Dottie's memory as a mostly unpleasant experience, but it did not deter her from taking on further running challenges. In the same month as the first River Run, Dottie and George participated in their first full marathon:

Our first marathon was run in Gainesville, middle Florida, in March 1978. It was a day of surprising heat and high humidity, a day when no one should run a marathon but be at the beach soaking in the ocean.

We woke up hot and humid at 5:30 in the morning. It was very, very hot: oppressive. The race started at 7:00 or 8:00 a.m. but could have started at 4:00 or 5:00 a.m. and it wouldn't have made much difference.

When it's your first race, and a big one, sometimes the warning signs are ignored. What do I remember? For the first time having to make a "pit stop" and there were no port-o-lets. It was—do it at the side of the road when no one was in sight. The "Long Day's Journey" to the finish looked like a MASH unit had just arrived with the wounded.

Hundreds of heat-exhausted bodies lined the entire finish area. Fortunately, the hospital was nearby, and they sponsored the event.

Would we ever run another marathon? The answer should have been a resounding "NO," but it wasn't.

Many marathons followed and New York City is always a highlight. We both ran it in 1979. When friends ask, "What is the best way to see N.Y.C.?" I always answer, "Run the New York City Marathon." It's the only race where I ever got three proposals for marriage, and one from a pink rabbit!

It's quite possible that Dottie and Celeste crossed paths unknowingly in the days and hours before and after the 1979 New York City Marathon. Celeste had not yet attempted a marathon. She was not in New York with intentions to compete in 1979; in fact, she had not even contemplated doing a marathon. But her fortuitous visit to the city at that point in time proved to be pivotal:

In late fall 1979 Dick and I were in New York City for a business trip.

As we looked out onto the streets during cocktails, I saw a lot of people wandering around and wondered why. The comment was made at the table that this was the weekend for the New York City Marathon.

Heavy sentence, that.

Immediately, as in "at that moment," I had to have the tee shirt.

"I want to sign up," I said. I knew I could probably run five miles. Then I could just go to Bloomingdale's. But I would have a killer tee shirt.

"You can't." From across the table. A dash of déjà vu scattered a couple of paper napkins.

"Too hard?"

"Too late. You have to apply before June, get drawn from a box, and then you can go."

"Oh."

So back in South Dakota, I told Jan that we were going to run a marathon in one year's time. Twenty-six point two miles. We had, at that time, run only just under five.

"OK."

And that was that.

On December 31 we planned that, on New Year's Day, we would begin our training. We would run our first six miles. At the party we drank Seven Up.

The next morning while most of Sioux Falls nursed its headaches, we trotted along the freshly shoveled bike path that eventually circled town. I can still see the tiny hairs on Jan's face, outlined in frost.

That was the beginning of a new adventure. We had a shared goal. That moment changed my life.

There was nothing written then about how to run a marathon. There were no trainers that we knew of. I don't recall picking up information from running magazines. Maybe I was too headstrong to seek information. I just decided to run and see if I could.

So we made up our own schedule. Worried about becoming lax, we stuck to that schedule as though it were a marriage contract. We would increase our mileage as I, the leader, chose to write it down. One day a week, we would get a sitter and run the long run. We would do the same length four weeks in a row, at ten-minute miles. I figured it out so that we were running twenty-three miles right before the race. The other days we would just run some threes when our big kids came home from school. I guess that one was our first of few mistakes. We should have had a middle-sized run each week. But our eyes were on the big run that increased month by month.

So we progressed. One April day, we drove clothes out of town to a luncheon venue, drove home, and then ran the eight miles to the party, showering and changing there, and somehow getting home. Summer came and we would run at night to stay out of the heat. We figured out that, if water were offered during a 5K, we would need some during our training. There was nothing then in which to carry water. So sometime during the day of the long run, we would drive to various spots along the bike path and hide a filled Mason jar. I am not sure we had graduated to peeing outside yet, in spite of all the woods through which we ran. But at approximately five-mile intervals, we sipped some water—re-collecting the jars the next day.

I loved the long, long runs. And the conversations. It was meditative. We would run the periphery of the woods and it would change. We saw the spring flowers. It was extraordinary.

I still played tennis.

But one day in August we were to do our first eighteen miles and someone from the tennis courts called to say I had to show up to try out for the new number ranking system. He said there was one day only to do this, so I said, "I quit." It was the beginning of my empowerment.

It is important to note Celeste's wording—why does she use the word "empowerment" for the first time in this context? Why not when she first ran around the block, or completed her first fun run? To me, it seems that quitting tennis went beyond the metaphorical exploration of a new golf course. It represents the beginnings of an explicit rejection of the golf course for which Celeste felt she had been prepared during her childhood and teenage years.

Celeste describes numerous instances of personal growth during her metamorphosis into marathon runner:

Jan was a sweet girl who was non-aggressive to her husband. She would not speak her needs. She did not present her needs. I had to learn to listen to her. She had four kids. Running was fun for her, but it was very hard trying to fit it in. She didn't believe in pampering herself. One time it was 25 degrees below zero. She put a baby behind glass, so the baby was warm, and then ran four laps around the block and back past her door to see if the baby was OK.

One summer evening, Jan commented toward a mid-fifteen miler that she felt a little sick. She had served some Mexican food, she said, for supper. It was not sitting well. She commented a couple more times that she felt sick. But we never let up. We did not know how. We did not abort the run; we never thought that was an option. About a block from my house, we finished the fifteen. Jan staggered over behind a well-placed bush and threw up. Hardheadedness was part of the deal. Thou shalt not be a wuss.

We learned a lot about ourselves that summer. We learned that after shorter runs, we were not hungry. After longer ones, we could eat a refrigerator. And we were, indeed, disciplined. Such was the *sine qua non* of the achievement of things lofty.

One day I mused that the reason that men could have key jobs in business is because they played sports. Men could go out and beat each other up at tennis and then sit down for a beer and chat. Women couldn't do that. Men could take a goal that was slightly over their heads and work at it, bit by bit, and know that soon all would be within their reach. Sports did that. So did post graduate degrees, which were not generally open to women: med school, law school, business school. We, however, did not have the opportunity to be bigger than we were. And so, we weren't.

We worried, though, that we would not get accepted into the marathon. So, becoming brazen through the effects of training, I decided to act and not to wait to re-act. I called the New York Runners' Club. Fred Lebow himself actually answered the telephone. "Listen," he said. "We try to get runners from all across the country. We have never had women from South Dakota before. In fact, we have few women. Do not worry. You will be in the race."

Beyond Triathlon

We knew we had to put in an application. The registrations could not be posted before June 2, I recall. Or post marked. Catholic school experience had taught precision, and Jan found out that the first June 2 post mark would start at 5:00 a.m. The last June 1 would be midnight. We could mail letters right after. The next post mark would be slap-dab regulation.

That night I told Dick I was going to stay up to watch the news. I put my girls' bike out behind the garage. Jan went to bed with Dewey but got up, saying she was going to the bathroom. Just before midnight, she stopped on her bike in front of my house. No helmets, no lights—we rode downtown to post our mail. I remember being surprised at all the people up so early and having Jan remind me that they had not yet been to bed.

Those chosen would receive notice toward the end of June. The wait for the mailman was unadulterated drama. Jan called first. I stood at the elm in front of the house. My acceptance came a long ten minutes after hers.

So that's what rapture was. We had made a goal. We had announced the goal. We had begun to train toward the goal. The goal had accepted us. Now what was left—to complete the goal—was on us, and us alone.

On the day of our twenty-three-mile run, our longest, a month before the marathon, I had such a pain in my back that I asked that we stop at a park restroom. I am surprised today to realize that, in one year of running through all sets of circumstances, that *that* pain, my pain, I am embarrassed to admit, was the only thing to stop me. Like, I would not stop for Jan. The short break did not help, though. We carried on at the same pace. Once home, I called a doctor. He—this is the fall of 1980—said I was thirty-seven and too old to run. He gave me muscle relaxers.

On reading this, I realize that Celeste is throwing her readers another clue to the specific nature of the stories she and Dottie have to tell. Their stories are not just about gender. They are also about age. They are about being female and beyond their young adult years.

But Celeste takes her time to tell the story of her first marathon. One month out, back pain threatened to thwart her plan.

A few days later, a friend recommended a chiropractor. I blanched. But I knew the chiropractor from church. His mother had been my daughter's teacher. So I made an appointment. I walked in and snapped, "Don't touch me, but—." He examined me and told me what the issue was: an unstable fifth lumbar. He did a lumbar roll and I felt good. He said I would be able to run the marathon but that, from that point till the race, I was just to walk. I obeyed him.

Because I knew that once I crossed the finish line of that first marathon, my life would never be the same.

I would be able to do whatever it was I set out to do.

And that's what has happened.

Experience is dear. We pass through moments, unguided, and then we have something to tell those who come behind us. Like about race logistics. The night before the race, Jan and I shared a hotel room and Dick went off with Dewey and the spouses of others who were also there. We got up at four. I do not remember what we ate. I do remember that we put on fresh fingernail polish. We hustled to get the first bus that left the Lincoln Center at 5:30 a.m. for Staten Island so we could avoid the crowds vying for the buses later. We were at race start at 6:00 a.m. The race start was at 10:00. We did not bring food or water. We did bring, as did others, garbage bags against the cold. Someone did give out some sort of bread item and coffee. But mostly we just sat and waited.

Learning our lesson from our inaugural 5K, we stood at the back of the pack on the Verrazano Bridge, almost in Staten Island itself. We were hungry and cold. And already tired. It took us thirteen minutes to cross the start line and eight miles till we could full out run.

Two tender-gender moments I recall: in Brooklyn, a woman stepped off the curb with tears in her eyes. She grabbed my arm. "You do not know what this means to me," she managed. In Harlem, a huge black woman did same to curb. She shook a hot dog sized finger in my face. "You better make it over the finish line, *you hear me, honey?*" We had no idea at that moment of our places in women's history.

We finished. However, the glory quickly turned to anti-climax. It took a while for the husbands to find us—you do not say "meet you at the finish line" of the 18,000 person New York City marathon. And when we did find each other, we each went back to our proper hotel rooms while the men, hungover, napped. I wanted to call people. I wanted to talk. That night we went to dinner at the top of the, get this, World Trade Center. Chatter everywhere. But none directed to us. Finally, after an hour of cocktails, I said, voice low: "Can we order now? Jan and I have had nothing to eat since 4:00 this morning." I did not know enough then to be angry. My experience would remain mine. No three rousing cheers.

But there was one nice family moment of unexpected visibility: my five-year-old son Colin, who continued to be involved in all my sporting life, took a newspaper photograph of the marathon to kindergarten. "Here is the New York Marathon," he said. "And here's my mom—way back here."

For the record, our finishing time was 4:28. We had no projection, except before nightfall. We were pleased.

When the marathon was over, I was a celebrity. We garnered the respect of family and of friends, as well as the entire city of Sioux Falls. Everyone knew who we were and what we were trying to do. Once we ran out to the airport to bring back Dick's car. We found our jackets too warm. We stopped at a film kiosk on a street corner and asked the clerk to hold the jackets for a bit. She stayed open a half an hour later because we were longer getting back than we expected. Another time, a drop off was at a bank. Same thing.

There was a United States senator. I would get this phone call from his aide saying, "he would like to run with you this afternoon." He couldn't run as fast as the men, but I was well known. He could run with me and people would stop him to talk. The first time he ran with me, I told my husband "You won't believe who is in the shower."

Years later, for fun, I wrote a book about two women who set out to run the New York City marathon. An agent called me immediately on receiving it. She said it was the funniest thing she had ever read but that also it had made her cry. The book was never published, mainly because I would not go off course from what had happened and make the women have affairs. But she, from NEW YORK, said that the book had everything: "female bonding" and "glass ceiling." I had never before heard those expressions.

I learned something else: about mile seventeen in a marathon, I would think the world was about to end. The pain was insufferable. And then at mile eighteen, all would be OK again. I had never heard, as well, about "the wall." In later years when things would be a little, oh, I dunno, with Dick, I would just say to myself that I was not yet at the eighteenth mile. And sure, enough, a bit later, all was hunky dory. I still say the same when things are murky: I'm just before the eighteenth mile.

For both Dottie and Celeste, their first marathon represented simply another beginning, rather than the end of a journey. The beginning and the end did not neatly follow each other; the old and new lives overlapped. The past was not yet a legacy; it persisted in the present, as was apparent when Celeste competed in her next marathon at Duluth, Minnesota in June 1982:

I ran another marathon two years later.

4. The Odd Person Out

We figured, while Jan was training with me the next year for Grandma's Marathon in Duluth, that we had trained for New York at ten-minute miles. We trained, then, without trying, for Grandma's at eight-minute miles. I tutored myself—perhaps inaccurately, perhaps not—that time on the trail led to speed.

Parenthetically, I add that Grandma's taught me that sometimes things happen in spite of how well one plans. Due to the flu, a third of the participants were unable to start the event. I had it also but did not know till mile five that things were not going to be OK. About mile twenty, a spectator looked and said to her companion, "That one's not going to make it." Just before the finish line, with the world turning dark, I grabbed a spectator to come with me. She asked my name. I later heard that she told the medics that I said my name was Kelly.

I was taken to the hospital in an ambulance, traumatizing my three children and my husband. I had 107 degree temperature. I remember thinking as I lay there that my mother was really going to be angry if I died because of a marathon. In E.R. they soaked me in ice. The temperature went down to 94. I could hear all this hustling about as I began to regain reality. In the ambulance they'd cut off my N.Y.C. Marathon finisher's shirt, even though I asked them not to. I was so embarrassed by my time of 4:02. I had wanted so badly a 3:28. I kept trying to tell the medics what happened, that I was better than what it seemed. Then I heard one cry out, "We cannot get a pulse!" *But I was there. I was there and they thought I was dead!* I am astounded now, as I think back upon the time.

Back then, though, it was normal for me not to feel heard. Me to husband: "I have to go to the bathroom." Husband: "No, you don't."

I was a celebrity in Duluth Hospital. The doctor said there was not a lot of heat stroke patients that far north. Then he came in and said that I was one of the flu victims. They wanted me to stay longer, but Dick wanted to drive back to Sioux Falls. That was a Monday. On Friday night I had ten couples for dinner. Previously invited. Initially, I wanted to cancel. I did not have to go to the bathroom. Nope.

The personal journeys facilitated by the turn to running were far from over, metaphorically or in reality. Dottie also ran other marathons. But as her fiftieth birthday approached, she sought a challenge that was bigger still, to mark the occasion.

When I turned fifty it was suggested by our eldest son, Mark, that I do a milestone run on my birthday. Since our son is an ultramarathoner he suggested a "Little" twenty-four-hour run on the track. I should have known immediately what "little" really meant. Sy Mah, guru of these runs, set me up on a program, which was run five miles and rest for twenty minutes and just keep going for twenty-four hours.

The college track looked like "tent city." Everyone had their own "home" or a deck chair to rest on. It was fun starting off because no one was in a rush. No one toed the start line or waited with bated breath to click their start watch. The lap counters were on ready to keep track of the laps we all ran. It started out as a nice sunny day and everyone chatting and making acquaintances with old friends and meeting "new" folks. When day turns to dusk, and night arrives it is cold and LONG. The companionship made it bearable and the experienced participants had no end of entertaining stories. The food served trackside gave us something to look forward to. My fifty-mile mark came sooner than expected and a big cheer went up from my companions, now all my "new best friends." I felt good and kept running to a 100K and our son was picking up the pace every mile for a record. All in a day's journey to nowhere.

If you can do this surely you can do some other "unusual" events. More "unusual" events followed.

Meant to be the "ultimate achievement," the marathon was not enough for Dottie, and, as it turns out, for Celeste as well. Running met some of the needs and frustrations prompting their dissatisfaction with social tennis, but not all. Something was still missing, but the memoirs written by Dottie and Celeste take a long time to make their respective points.

5

In Search of Wildflowers

The "unusual events" that followed featured additional sporting disciplines. In the early 1980s, having learned to run, and challenged themselves subsequently to compete in marathons, Dottie and Celeste both heard about events that involved swimming, cycling and running. Neither Dottie nor Celeste could claim to have done anything other than pedal and splash for fun. Neither harbored a wish to excel at swimming and cycling. Neither imagined a sport that combined both with running in a single continuous race. Neither embarked on their respective sporting journeys with triathlon as the destination.

Celeste:

A few weeks after the Duluth marathon, while on a fun run, Jan said to me: "Do you know what they are doing in Hawaii?"

"Mmmm?"

"They are swimming two and a half miles in the ocean. They are biking 112 miles. And *then* they are doing a marathon."

I, who thought running a marathon was the ultimate achievement, said, "That's the stupidest thing I have ever heard."

"But," she went on, "In Topeka I hear there are shorter distances."

While neither planned to do so, both Celeste and Dottie decided to explore the trail marked "multisport" when they came across it. As the accounts of their first experiments with triathlon reveal, the respective reasons they put forward for attempting multisport diverge considerably, but as they narrate this new athletic phase, they highlight some common themes. In large part this is intentional. In planning to tell their stories jointly, they no doubt intended to draw out the similarities. But many of the parallels appear to exist naturally—implicitly—within the stories they tell.

Dottie's memoir launches into an account of her first triathlon, staged by the local YMCA [Y] in 1980, with little preamble or explanation:

Beyond Triathlon

I think it was advertised in a Jacksonville Track Club newsletter or at the Y. I also heard about a triathlon race from a friend and she said, "It will just be fun." I had a stress fracture from running and decided to give it a try.

I was more than a little worried since I really couldn't swim, only dog paddle and sidestroke. Does anyone even remember sidestroke? This was a low-key "Y" thing so I decided I could just grease up my three speed Schwinn, find my bike helmet and practice my dog paddle.

On race day we went to a rural location and leaned our bikes on a tree or just dropped them on the ground. The order of events was run, bike and then swim last in a pool. The run and bike went O.K. but the swim was a nightmare. The pool was "wall to wall" people and as I tried my primitive strokes, I thought I would drown. I swallowed grubby water and sputtered it out. Somehow you keep going. When I finally finished, I discovered I could have walked the whole pool length because it was really quite shallow. I was too afraid to even put my feet down. So there is a moral to this story.

In contrast, Celeste's account locates a growing interest in triathlon against a personal struggle with social dislocation and isolation. In this instance, the Callahan household, following Dick's work, moved from the American Mid-West to the North West. Among other things, the move threatened to disrupt the personal journey on which Celeste had embarked—her metaphorical exploration of a new, independently chosen golf course—which was, until then, tied firmly to her new found ability to run and a linked discovery of a different type of camaraderie with her running partner Jan.

Following their initial conversation about triathlon, Jan and Celeste set off down the intriguing new athletic trail together. Celeste recounts in her memoir:

So we began to practice. We would ride our girl bikes with baby seats on the back to the movies. We would then run. Running after biking was killer. We joined a masters swim team at the Y. She brought along her kids' goggles. I had never before worn goggles. Jan gave me some tips. I thought I had done pretty well. The coach corrected me heavily.

And then we moved to Seattle—Mercer Island actually—from Sioux Falls, South Dakota. Dick, starting a brand new invention called cellular telephony, was widely heralded. My children, in a new school, were adapting well. The two boys—in grade and middle school—were at that dumb joke phase, and the daughter was a bored high schooler.

No one paid me any mind. Like who would? I was just the mother. I would listen to the silent walls during the day, trying to define myself. I missed Jan. I missed that goal thing, having that out-of-reach goal to work for, as the marathon had given me. I joined a sports club and I would go in the evenings and try to swim a mile. I was determined.

I remember a single woman named Linda who had long, dirty, blond, unruly curls. She told me once that she'd "hung out" that weekend. I have for decades pondered that expression. "I hung out all weekend." Linda was everything I wanted to be. And I had everything in those days that she wanted, except my options. I would have traded my "real life" for hers, which was actually one that looked for mine. I just wanted to be able to say things like "I hung out." Or, as in another case, "the rhododendrons are early this year." People seemed to think for themselves, to be themselves. They were self-programmed. I was not. I was instead a catalogue made-for-order wife or mom.

One day in the Bellevue Athletic Club Bulletin there was an ad, next to one for Round Robin Bridge, to climb Mount Rainier—this 14,000-foot dome that sometimes we saw off our terrace and sometimes we didn't. So I called Jan. Sure, she said. And, independently, she in Sioux Falls and I on Mercer Island, entered and trained to climb Mount Rainier. For a spring, I pursued what would be called my brief mountaineering phase. I read all I could. I got one of the first editions of *Freedom of the Hills*, which is now a cool thing to say you've read. I visited the REI [*Recreational Equipment Inc.*] flagship store, a cultural experience for a mom. Dick and I did day hikes.

I read that a very good Mount Rainier training, ah, thing, would be to do an endurance event sometime before the two-day climb. Taking my kids to buy sports shoes one day, I saw a poster on a board for a triathlon to be held just over the Mercer Island Bridge in just one week.

"Read, fire, aim," my philosophy has always been. I signed up. Just like that. $25.00.

In July 1983, a year earlier, my daughter Kelly—about twelve—and I, had gone to watch the same triathlon. We woke up early to watch the swim start. I had to suppress a giggle: the sky was the color of attic insulation; it was chilly, and I just remember seeing everyone treading water with open mouths. And then the countdown. With everyone else, I yelled HOORAY. My daughter said, "Shh." So I did.

So it was Tuesday. July 3, 1984. I knew that triathlons started with the swim. But I had no further information. My triathlon was in six days. Five? Sunday. I lay on the floor looking at a grey sky without definition or variant in shade, framed in the glass door of our laundry room. I looked at the top corner of the dryer. Somewhere I saw a tree branch. My stomach churned like a Cuisinart processor. I had never been this afraid. Afraid of what? I did not know. I think it was the swim. I think it was the beginning of the swim. I had no idea how to do a triathlon. I had no clue what was expected, except to swim a distance that had a seven in it. I had to bike maybe twelve miles. Maybe twenty-five. I had no idea. I had to run a 10K. That I could do. But I had entered without any inkling of what was expected of me or if I could manage.

On Wednesday, July 4, at a neighbors' place, I put my head into the water of Lake Washington. I was so surprised that there were no lights down there, no long blue line. Just floating *things*, many of them green.

My neighbor had a canoe. I asked if she would take me to the race site and follow me. I wanted to see if I could swim, or what the swim would feel like. She was to follow me along a course that began in the water and crossed to the other side of the lake, where the bikes would be.

I headed off.

Conk.

And then another conk.

I looked up. "You are swimming in circles," she called.

"Oh."

My husband did not want to me do this triathlon. "You will be too tired to cook for us," he said, his face straight. So I planned to do the event, go to the grocery store, cook and clean up. Which I did, as it turns out. But I had no idea what this would feel like.

The day before the race, I went to the race site for a meeting. Someone shouted the instructions, none of which I understood. A magazine article was handed out. I spent an hour reading it when I got home. It told what to do in a triathlon. It explained a transition. I got ready.

Celeste made it through her first triathlon, and describes feeling a small rush of satisfaction, but it was little more than a means to an end and another novel tee shirt:

So we "did" Mount Rainier. I knew that I picked a very dangerous thing. It was hard. There were no microfiber clothes, and my wool Navy store pants itched. We had to wear rain suits. I had my period. I took a lot of abuse from the Rainier Mountaineering guides whose job is—not to get you up the mountain—but to get you down. So they try to intimidate those who they think will not make it.

I am short.

I was cute.

5. In Search of Wildflowers

I was target.

One of the things they did the first day—Friday—is try to scare you off. People die up there. They teach you how to use an axe. They would get you to slide down a hill and turn around and use an axe to stop yourself. We were told how to breathe to get oxygen to our legs and heads. I thought for Jan it might have been too much. She wasn't equal to me in terms of drive and anger.

We climbed on the Saturday. At night nobody could sleep. At midnight they looked at the weather and then said, "We're going now."

I made it. We made it. We had some fun and we had some laughs. We couldn't go down steps the next day and it was months before I could look at a picture of pristine mountains and valley wildernesses without wanting to throw up. Or the lemon drops that we sucked on by the dozens for a reason that now I cannot remember.

However, it was not a marathon. I crossed off another goal. But I did not think that one counted. We only trained for a few weeks. It wasn't a dream I had for a very long time. I didn't have that yen, didn't live there a long time. I thought it would be a quick fix, but it was not something I could practice every Thursday. And I didn't think I had business up there because I had children. When it was over, I was still where I was. It felt like, maybe, an extra paragraph in the story of my life—one that would, maybe, end up on the cutting room floor.

Celeste clarifies reflexively that the Mount Rainier climb is not key to the central story of the memoir. It only explains why she participated in her first triathlon. The first triathlon appears as a means to an end, but the "end," was not the peak of a mountain. If Celeste's confessed admiration for the woman who "hung out all weekend" is any guide, the real end goal might have more to do with a state of mind than a specific physical challenge, with having a sense of self, rather than the reality of pushing her physical limits.

Mountaineering disappeared as an interest as soon as Celeste returned to sea level. And for a year it might have seemed to family and friends that triathlon represented a one-off means to an end as well, as fleeting as mountain climbing on the checklist of cures for restlessness. But in the fall of 1985, serendipity—and whatever internal processes prompted her to tackle Washington State's soaring volcanic peak—combined to inspire Celeste to undertake a second multisport challenge.

Sometime later I saw another sign, again at the Bellevue Athletic Club [*BAC*]: "Triathlon Club."

I decided to talk to the person behind the desk that bore the sign.

Beyond Triathlon

Knowing what I know now, it seems ludicrous and extravagant that a private sports club would hire a full-time triathlon coach and give him an actual office. Todd was his name, and he was adorable as well as the epitome of "cool." This sort of fellow was outside my ken: a man, maybe in his twenties, talking to me as though I were a person with a border that held me in and others out. He said he had watched me swim one evening when I was acting out on what Jan had said about what they were doing in Hawaii. As it turns out, he had been watching someone else. But the error gave me enough bravura to sign my name for an $18 charge on my BAC bill each month.

So the new long-term goal was there. From November to next July I would train several days a week with this group of, maybe, twenty five young men and women—a few women, many men—for the same triathlon I had already done with no training, no instruction and no idea as to how to navigate myself through about twenty five miles of unfamiliar terror.

Good. Just what I needed.

My days consisted of getting kids to school, carpooling Colin who better thrived, we found out, at a costly Episcopalian primary across the bridge than at the Catholic one right there on the island. I would then clean up the house. We did have a cleaning lady, who came every two weeks. But I did my straightening thing. The laundry. I would work on magazine articles, selling some. And then I would go to noon swim practice. Every day consisted of some form of work out. And then it was time to collect children, attend their sporting activities, and prepare dinner. I felt a bit like a Colossus of Rhodes with one foot on one island and the other on the next. But soon it was 1986, and seven months till the triathlon.

Having scattered clues through her accounts of young adulthood, of playing tennis, and learning to run, Celeste's story of her first triathlon feels—to me—like she is finally hinting as to where her path through the metaphorical forest leads. Her tales come across as allegories for a journey of self-discovery. At last the heroine has begun to move on from narratives of dissatisfaction and searching. Finally flashes of light cut through the shadows; now there are glimmers of self-awareness and clarity.

Athletic goals gave Celeste something distinct from her husband and children, something that separated her from them and rendered her as a unique individual. Dottie provides fewer clues as she recounts the story of her first triathlon but reveals more when she attempts to explain why her first triathlon was not her last. As always, she returns to the deep past and places her clues strategically.

I became quite intrigued with the possibility of triathlon. Even with a disastrous start I liked the idea of an event with three different entities and knowing that if one aspect of the three didn't go well you could look forward to the next one. In running, if things did not go well, it was just one long struggle to the finish line.

Many family and friends asked me, "How did you become so determined, maybe even stubborn, to continue to pursue new and different 'activities'?"

Sometimes I go back to my experience as a Girl Scout. First I was a proud Brownie, but the real pride came in being a Girl Scout. Perhaps it was the new uniform, not a hand-me-down, and later with all the badges sewn on? Kind of like putting on your safety patrol belt at grade school maybe? Most special of all was that my mom was our troop leader. I busied myself earning badges to make her proud and me too. My hardest-to-earn badge was a wildflower badge, which consisted of finding and identifying fifty wildflowers. My parents were so pleased to have my hyperactivity funneled to spending hours searching for wildflowers in fields and neighbors' yards. When we went on car trips I would be yelling, "Stop! I see some wildflowers I don't have."

Girl Scouts taught me about "teamwork" at an early age and that by co-operating with other scouts we could accomplish a goal together. It was not just about "Me."

When I went to my first sleepover camp, after I got over my homesickness, I loved the outdoor activities, especially the many different sports. It was the first time I felt the camaraderie of sharing experiences with like minds. Sitting around a campfire at night and making s'mores was a treat. Even if most of the marshmallows either burned black or had nothing left after they peeled down and dropped into the fire.

Most of all was marching in the 4th of July parades. My mom was leading our troop and I was dressed in my uniform, neat as a pin. The crowds cheering us on only added to "Our" sense of importance. One year I even got to carry the American flag and I was afraid the whole route that "My" flag would touch the ground and that was a huge "no no."

I attribute this experience to an early start to my athletic career and beginning to understand that girls, when given the opportunity, can achieve certain goals either single or with "teams."

This anecdote suggests that Dottie, too, places importance on goals.

But by co-opting the past in an effort to explain her attraction to triathlon, Dottie reveals that she had learned to chase pre-existent goals. They were framed largely by her mother, but also by convention, and by the Girl Scout movement.

The individual sports of running and triathlon offered both Dottie and Celeste the opportunity to set and strive for goals—of their own volition—which had not been set by parents, partners, the Catholic Church, or the Girl Scouts. Possibly the key difference between the ways in which Dottie and Celeste approached the notion of goal setting, was that Dottie had grown up with the taste of achievement, of setting, pursuing and reaching goals, while Celeste had only sampled, belatedly, the sweet rewards of accomplishment. Previously Celeste simply met expectations.

It is perhaps not surprising that, as the memoirs drafted by Dottie and Celeste turn to their athletic experiments, particularly their efforts to master triathlon, their accounts begin to converge. Both proceed to describe key aspects of their transformation into triathletes—in particular their struggle to master the new sports of swimming and cycling.

Dottie continues:

Back to my determination to learn to swim which is a very technical sport and extremely difficult to learn at an "advanced" age (forty-six to be exact). I had to realize that although you can bike and run, it has no connection to swimming. My first swim lessons were at the local Y. The instructor had all the participants line up on the end of the pool and shouted, "Jump in." I immediately went to the bottom of the pool. Everyone else was floating on the top. This was not good news and I knew this was a whole new world of sport. The instructor then said, "Swim one lap." Well, I didn't know what one lap meant: was it one length or two? I could barely go one length and ended up hanging onto the pool and crying my eyes out. The instructor proceeded to tell me to do so many things at one time I was totally confused and very frustrated. I got out of the pool in tears and, dripping wet, went to my car and drove home.

Celeste, too, struggled when she first sought proper swimming instruction, and spent many hours in the pool, working to improve:

The training adventures are a long story. At the first swim workout, I was laughed at. Really. A fellow named Quinn. Red head. Would love for him to see me now. The coach put me in the C lane with the other beginners. Plus older people. He also suggested that I come three days a week and not the two that I thought would carry me through.

So I swam three days a week at the BAC. I even began to enjoy myself. I never made much progress, but fellow swimmers shouted

"Good job!" as though I were in the Special Olympics. I liked that my efforts were noticed. No sob story here. I think my children were happy with me. It's just that there are no praises for soccer game rides that do not involve an accident.

Acquiring the requisite knowledge, fitness and skills for the bike leg of a triathlon proved more complicated. She did not know anything about gears or the type of bike that most triathletes, even then, chose to ride. Nor did Celeste know how to change a tire, to train, or to draft (ride close to the wheel of another rider for the relief and the assistance gained in the leader's slipstream). There were no coaches for cycling in the same way that there were for swimming. And the purchase and maintenance of equipment remained the responsibility of the individual cyclist. Celeste received some guidance from the paid Bellevue Athletics Club (BAC) triathlon coach, but not a lot.

At the first bike workout, I showed up with my same girls' Schwinn with basket. I looked at all the sleek neon colored aluminum and steel steeds others were riding. Todd said that we would try to stay in a 20mph pace line. I said I did not think this bike would go that fast. Not to mention me. Thinking back, I bet I had no gears. The bike. Anyway, I lasted a block.

In parenthesis, I recall that the next week I bought a new bike. Here is how I bought this new bike: I went into a bike store on Mercer Island.

"I am looking for a bike for a triathlon," I said.

She asked me some questions that I must have gotten wrong. She pointed to a green Bianchi for about $350.

"This is a good entry level triathlon bike," she said.

"I'll take it," I said.

And I did. I did not test drive it. I did not have it fitted. I did not have a changing gears tutorial. I just took it. I drove it home. In my Chrysler LeBaron station wagon. I put it in the garage. A week later, I took it around the island, which, if you know Mercer Island, Washington, consists of a perimeter of thirteen miles of nine to thirteen percent grade hills. It took me an hour to make the round. Actually, more like two days. I hated it. But I got on that bike three to four times a week and rode Mercer Island Way, East to West. Sometimes I got up to fifteen miles an hour. But I hated it. I hated it.

The bike back then: I just needed time on it. Come spring was the STP, the Seattle to Portland 200-mile ride. Or race. The racers, really, did the 200 in one day. Many from our club did the same. The rest of us did 100 one day and 100 the next. A large woman, Linda, who worked at the club doing—I do not remember what—took pity on me, sort of like the physics nun, and let me ride her wheel. The longest I had gone before that day was thirty-four miles. Three of us had driven to a park about two weeks before the event and ridden the thirty-four after which I wanted to lie down in the parking lot and die. On the way home that day, I stopped at Jack in the Box for a hamburger and fries. At home, I cooked an entire family dinner and promptly ate my share. I would not have gotten to Portland without Linda. The other woman, named Caroline, had a flat before we left Seattle. Linda left her. I said, "But if I have a flat? ..."

"I would not leave you," she called back against the wind.

I was in no position to argue the merits of justice or fair play.

And on we rode, stopping only briefly at the rest stops provided by the ride. We got to our first destination, halfway, just before supper. We checked into a motel, several of us. We bathed. We went out to eat everything we could get our hands on. We got up the next day and did it again. And all I saw for the fourteen hours of riding over two days was the hub of Linda's rear wheel.

No one said anything to me about *training* for the STP ... about going out for rides of forty and then fifty and then sixty, over and over and over again. God must love fools and children. He sent me Linda who I never saw before this adventure. Or after.

Noting the lack of instruction for triathletes—women triathletes in particular—Dottie learned about cycling through experience as well:

There were so few resources for us on triathlon, one magazine, and several books on running. There were two books on running for women, Councilman's book on swimming, and Kenneth Cooper's book on fitness. We mostly learned by "Trial and Error" and "Flew by the Seat of Our Pants."

My next challenge was to get on my new ten speed bike and ride with "the Big Boys," from the local bike shop. One early morning ride we were cruising along, warming up, when I had a drippy nose. I simply reached into the back pocket of my new bike shirt, pulled out my white lace handkerchief and started to blow my nose. The next thing I knew all the riders had dropped back to witness me blowing my nose. Great peals of laughter ensued because that is NOT the way it is done on the bike!

Bringing the three disciplines together, both women began to work toward their first proper attempts at triathlon: Celeste's second Seafair Triathlon at Seattle in 1986, and Dottie's first President's Triathlon at Dallas in 1984. Celeste began to enjoy training with the triathlon club,

Dottie competing in a triathlon in the 1980s, wearing a new Bell helmet and riding a ten speed Quintana Roo bike with toe clips (courtesy George Dorion).

although inevitably she felt most comfortable training for the final triathlon discipline—the run:

For the run: I just ran. I ran mostly with the taciturn husband of a friend, he a convert to the Catholic Church. I told him if he did not start talking as we ran, I would recite the rosary. I was beginning to have fun with my life, coloring outside the lines.

The running, though, has good memories. My best is a cold evening at a 7:00 p.m. track practice when the coach had us doing mile repeats. I ran with a small group of men. We were silent. The air was crisp. The stars twinkled as they do to a child who has just been allowed to stay up past dark. You could hear our footfalls. You could see our breath. I matched them step for step for spot-on seven-minute miles. That was a moment that forever lives deep inside my soul. I had pulled out something I had no idea was there.

The year went by. I began to like the noonday swims, three days a week. I began to have friends, both women and men. I liked the club idea. There would be a club 10K, and I would finish first among masters females, and there would be no end to the slaps on the back. Plus, a $50 bill as prize, which I threw across the kitchen counter to Dick as he talked on the phone. As in "AHA!"

After a while, I did really enjoy the workouts; I considered them an interruption to a day that was going nowhere anyway. But I was not one of the gang, although I bonded with a few of the folk—the girl who "hung out," for instance. I did not feel that triathlon, or this group, was my thing. I was not sure what my thing was. I liked teaching. I liked being a mother to younger children, and I liked writing. While I enjoyed exercise to some degree—and always loved running—I did not feel that biking long hours or driving across Mercer Island Bridge to Bellevue to swim for an hour was a good use of my time. I did not feel it *led* to anything except for one last try at the ladder that offered a way over the walls that held me in. My goal was a second try, as I said, at the mottled event that I had used as preparation for climbing Mount Rainier—that, too, a road that led to nowhere as I tried to figure out, not knowing that I was doing so, who in the hell I was.

One cloudy afternoon Dick called long distance from some place or another. He began his story as he begins all his messages, skipping only the Dark and Stormy Night bit. He told me that, as I know, Northwestern Bell is now part of a bigger company, US West, and that he has been head of US West Cellular and that, *now*, he has been asked to head what will be called US West International—working on fiber optic cable and cellular projects all over the world.

I stood at the sofa at which I had been sitting. I waited.

"So." He said. "We will move to Denver." The next part came fast. "We will leave in June as soon as the kids are out of school."

I did not hesitate.

"I can't," I said.

"What?" Or something like that.

"I have to do this goddamn triathlon."

A noise of *oh, small details, this.* "OK. When is the triathlon?"

5. *In Search of Wildflowers*

"July 20."

"OK. We will leave.... July 22nd."

And we both hung up the phone. That is the way we met with life changes. He would call. I would say OK. And then there would begin the process of smoothing things over for the children, selling one house and buying yet another, and standing in a new line at a DMV.

Only this time I had put me first. And there was no real opposition. Who knew?

I stood; phone in hand, for just a moment, staring out at the steel grey bit of Lake Washington that undulated down the hill in front of the neighbor's house below.

So there it was again—the athletic goal gave Celeste a reason to push back, to resist the destiny for which she felt she had been groomed.

For both Dottie and Celeste, having decided to continue with the triathlon experiment, it seemed important to do it with hopes of—at the very least—avoiding embarrassment, and potentially of doing much better. Each woman prepared seriously for her first proper attempt at a major triathlon. Yet, as Dottie explains, that involved more than acquiring simply the capacity to swim and ride a bike:

My first "BIG" triathlon was the President's Triathlon in Dallas Texas in 1984. I chose the short course because I considered it doable for me, or so I thought.

The bike shop boxed up my bike and showed me how to put it together. I never trained to be a bike mechanic and reluctantly tried to learn the trade, which was essential for triathlon. I still think that dealing with all sizes of Allen wrenches, hand bike pumps, changing tires and putting chains back on are all miserable chores. The tool kit you Must have was a complete enigma to me.

And just to travel with a bike is a pain. It never comes out on the belt with your suitcase, but from a door in the back of the unload area. The rental car needs space for the bike and, of course, in 1984 I didn't know to plan ahead for that.

Even after I had my bike and rental car, it was a challenge to get maps and find my way to the hotel and race headquarters. The carbo-loading dinner the night before was fine for seasoned triathletes who had no fears and just kept eating and eating. We, fledgling newcomers, picked at the food with nervous stomachs that were not very accepting of food due to our anxiety over the next day's race.

The start of what was to become a very difficult day began with the wind howling and the lake swim waves were at least ten feet tall, in my mind's eye, of course. The waves were also coming in the wrong direction since I could only breathe on one side, doing sidestroke, and I started swallowing copious amounts of not so clean water. Next I was vomiting, and the rescue boat was alongside me and the crew was at first inviting me aboard and then shouting for me to get in now! I started pleading with them between gulps and sobs to just "let me finish." I did finish the swim, dead last, no surprise. The rest of the race went well, and I was proud to finish.

In her memoirs and oral accounts Celeste identifies feelings of both ambivalence and determination when describing her second attempt at the Seafair Triathlon. She still felt uncertain about whether triathlon meant anything for her personally, but determined, as well, to strive for the goal she had set for herself. She was committed enough to disrupt the usual pattern of moving house according to the work needs of her husband. Her memoir account continues:

The triathlon. I was really going to do it. And then we would move. And then I would continue with the post in which life had placed me. Shepherding others toward their dreams. Mine were met, after all.

Triathlon day was coming. I did a practice one with friends about three weeks before. Everyone should try something about which she knows absolutely nothing. This friend, Caroline, met me at the BAC and I rode with her to this "practice" race which was a real race that I used as a training tool. I do not remember any pre-race angst or meal. I remember, most of all, the long wait for the swim. I would fight the frigid water—just fifty something degrees—with a neoprene swim cap. One woman in my age group had a short-sleeved rubber outfit that reached not quite to her knees. But wet suits were not available then. That was triathlon in those days. A leader or manager or director would choose a day and a course, and we would all hand over our money and sign our names and just do it. Now we have words like "ambient air." We did not know it back in Seattle in the '80s, that what we were doing would one day be illegal and hazardous to our ability to exit the race alive.

Our tri team did an open water swim one evening, but by the time I found them, they were done. At my only other practice, the coach followed me—the only female and the last—in a canoe. The water was about fifty-three degrees. Again. So was the air. Also. The others shivered in towels waiting for me to finish. I always remember that day when today I think the water will be too cold. In almost thirty years, it never has been as cold.

I got out of the water just as Caroline was tying her shoes: "Hey, great swim," she offered. My bike was parked against a tree, I think. I did not know how to set up transition. No one did. I do remember I used a shoehorn to help my frozen feet get into the shoes in which I would bike and run; I did not see my first bike cleats [*mechanisms that attach to the bottom of cycling shoes to allow them to clip into matching attachments to the pedal*] 'til weeks later.

I rode the bike. A man with a baby seat on the back passed me. I had no finish goal except not to fall and not to flat. The latter was the larger concern. "Please, God, do not let me flat," was to become my prayer for the next five years until one day someone said: "Celeste. God does not care whether or not you get a flat tire in a race." Anyway, as I was coming into the transition, I saw Caroline take off on the run. It was the first time I thought about placement in this sport. In short, I knew I had her.

I passed her in mile one. She did not show up for another race with me in it. Again.

The practice triathlon may have afforded Celeste some encouragement, chiefly in the form of confidence in her ability to run well after swimming and cycling, but the prospect of competing in the Seafair Triathlon still remained daunting.

The week of the Seafair, my goal triathlon, provided for me the understanding with which to coach over one thousand women, something I would do much later. I felt like an inmate on Death Row, each morning getting me closer to The End. There are not too many memories of the event. It was a pretty day. The swim, I bet, was about half a mile. I think, as I look back, the literature said 750 meters. I had no concept of an acceptable time. As before, I stood on the banks and waited 'til the gun went off. Tom, our swim coach at the water exit yelled, "Good swim, Celeste!" A clock said something like "00:45." I am guessing that was my time and that we had just one wave. Today I would swim 750 meters in under fifteen minutes. Today, the race would have ended with me still in the lake with that kind of time. But triathlon in those days was comprised of disenchanted runners. I was not the only one who did not know what to do or how to do it. There is little connection between swimming in a pool and doing the same in a cold, dark, murky lake.

The bike? OK. No flat. I had a crowd around me the whole time, which means I shared some ability somehow.

The run. I remember passing several women in my age group. We wore our age on our calves.

When I crossed the finish line, I ran into the open arms of my cute coach Todd. I remember the morning sun piercing through the trees into

In 1986, not all triathlons had bike racks, and competitors took a little more time in transition. Here, Celeste wrestles to put her shoes on after the swim (Celeste Callahan Private Collection).

my eyes as I hugged him. I knew I was moving to Denver in forty-eight hours. "I'm done!" I cried. "No more training!" I heaved aside one of life's heaviest burdens. I had challenged myself and I had come out the better.

By completing their first respective serious attempts at triathlon, Dottie and Celeste accomplished something well beyond the tennis-playing versions of themselves. It was not just that they mastered at least the bare basics of the additional skills of swimming and cycling, or that they were much fitter. In their memoirs both suggest that feelings of satisfaction arose from the process of striving for and achieving their novel athletic goal.

Wearing a Bellevue Athletic Club sweatshirt and carrying her clip-in pedals, Celeste looks relieved and pleased in the wake of the first triathlon for which she trained as an event in its own right, the 1986 Seafair Triathlon (Celeste Callahan Private Collection).

But what was next? Celeste faced another round of adjustment to a new home and neighborhood, of finding something for herself that was not linked to those for whom she cared. Dottie was not committed necessarily to triathlon. No one expected them to continue. Although women were competing in running events in greater numbers by the mid–1980s, understandings of age and physical fitness led most event organizers to designate competitors in the over thirty-five age group as "veterans."

Beyond Triathlon

A fifty-year-old woman represented as much a novelty, an aberration, as the multisport events Dottie and Celeste had just completed. Shouldn't, wouldn't, the respective triathlons they undertook in the summers of 1984 and 1986 represent—as Celeste put it—an "End" in themselves?

6

A Giant Enchilada

Of course, the 1984 President's Triathlon was not Dottie's last multisport event. Nor was the 1986 Seafair Triathlon "the end" for Celeste.

In part, the motivation to continue related to the timing of the respective multisport endeavors undertaken by Dottie and Celeste. Awareness of what was viewed previously as a novelty sport had increased dramatically due to Wide World of Sports *coverage of the Hawaiian ultradistance triathlon known as Ironman.[1] The leading woman in the February 1982 Budweiser Light Ironman World Triathlon, Julie Moss, collapsed as she entered the finish chute at Kailua-Kona. Television footage captured her struggle to control her failing legs, and final desperate effort to crawl to the finish line; all while Kathleen McCartney, the woman in second place, ran past her to claim the win. For many reasons the footage captured the attention of viewers. It was played over and over around the world, bringing the triathlon concept to the attention of a global audience and inspiring a wave of enthusiasm for multisport events.*

At the same time that Dottie and Celeste learned to ride and swim, triathlon enthusiasts were laying the foundations of the sport. In the United States, a national race series took hold, while others established a national governing body, seeking to introduce a sense of law and order. They were already talking about Olympic recognition.

This context impacted inevitably on the next athletic goals that

---

1. Ironman branding requires that the word Ironman be used as an adjective for IRON-MAN® branded events. The requirements were not in place at the time that Dottie and Celeste, and many others, first set their goals to compete in the ultradistance event at Hawaii. In triathlon vernacular, the word Ironman is used as a noun to refer to both the event and any individual who completes the event. In annotations, the term is used as an adjective, and branding requirements are observed when reference is made to specific Ironman events. Where the word Ironman appears in the memoirs drafted by Dottie and Celeste, it is presented as they use it, without alteration. For further information about IRONMAN® branding requirements, please see: IRONMAN®, "Brand Guidelines," 2020, https://www.ironman.com/brand-guidelines.

Dottie and Celeste set for themselves. Dottie was pleased to have finished the 1984 President's Triathlon, but the experience left her with a desire to do better:

The celebration was fun, and I made up my mind to return the following year for the longer course.

The next year I did return after some excellent swim instruction with a Masters Swim Team and a good coach. I got a coach for my swim stroke, a young man who qualified for the Olympics as a swimmer, and I swam five to ten thousand meters every day, being mindful that I had to do "the crawl" no matter how difficult. It was helpful that I didn't have a lot of bad swim habits and I could conquer one technique at a time. I was really excited when I moved from the lane marked "SLOW" to "MODERATE." The "FAST" lane was still doing twice the number of laps it took me to do one. I was certain that my skintight Speedo bathing suit was helping me, now that my ruffled number was gone—forever. I'm very proud of my swimming, getting one thing under control at a time.

I felt really ready for this BIG race and I was determined, or as my husband says, "Stubborn."

Look out Dallas! Here I come!

The 1985 President's Triathlon was on one of the hottest days on record. The sun beat down the entire race and it was so dry the dust balls curled around my body. It was over 100 degrees and I never stopped, just grabbing water along the way. I finished the race beating my next competitor by 1 hour and 58 minutes.

That race was a qualifier for The Hawaii Ironman. Back in 1982 I saw Ironman on TV—I saw Julie Moss crawl across the finish line and thought I'd really like to do an Ironman if I could swim and bike. At the President's Triathlon awards ceremony, I waited impatiently for my name to be announced and my Ironman Qualifying slot to be awarded. I carried the letter for "my slot" with me for two weeks because I was troubled and very indecisive. The thought of an Ironman was overwhelming. I had nightmares about how my family would fare. Work, and other commitments would have to be compromised for me to put in the training necessary. I wasn't sure I was willing to sacrifice those responsibilities and decided I only wanted to do it if my husband supported me. Finally, with the support of my husband and children, I said, "YES."

Dottie qualified for her first Ironman triathlon in the summer of 1985. Although she competed in the "long course" President's Triathlon to earn her slot, it was still less than half the distance of her new athletic goal, which boasted a 2.4 mile ocean swim, 112 mile bike ride and full marathon—a 26.2 mile run—all in continuous succession. And she had only four months to prepare.

Watching Julie Moss finish the Hawaii Ironman did NOT boost my confidence, as in my first Ironman I would be twice her age! We had few resources to guide us. We had one triathlete magazine. They had listed a training schedule for a 1.5K swim, 40K bike and a 10K run, today called "the Olympic distance." Being really ignorant I decided to just triple the training they gave. I proceeded to swim at least 5 miles, bike 150 and run 40–50 per week.

I learned a very important lesson. When there is a task that is absolutely overwhelming, a giant enchilada, just break it down into manageable segments. Instead of anguishing over the whole task, just break it down into parts. This ensures you take just one step at a time. Just plan to train day by day, which becomes weeks and weeks, and month by month, and voila ... it becomes "the Day."

But while training for "the Ironman" in 1985 a very unexpected occurrence took place. We wanted to build a house with accommodation for our parents and bought some land at Amelia Island, north of Jacksonville, and started clearing the trees for the house foundations. When he was digging up the palm trees, the backhoe operator found bones, bones and more bones. Too many to be a coincidence.

My husband and I thought, "How will we do this?" Several friends said cover it over and build your house, but we knew we might have a mission site because it was mentioned in literature previously. We also felt very strongly that once the ruins were destroyed and a house built over them, they would be lost forever. An archaeologist was contacted to discern what the bones were and to advise us. I must admit, what he discovered was a big surprise as it turned out they were human remains. It was obviously a graveyard.

We began to excavate the area with the help of some volunteer archaeologists, but the site turned out to be very extensive. So then we opened it up for school and college students from all over, so they could see what the archaeologists were doing. Around two thousand students visited during the eight and a half years it took to excavate the entire acreage. It was exciting to discover that our entire property was the St Catalina de Guale Mission site, which dated from 1684 to 1702. We found the remains of 150 or more Guale Indians, then the church, the convent, and casina. We even found civil war artifacts, which we donated to different places. Another artifact was the remarkable seal that the Bishop used on all of his letters, which we donated to a museum in Miami.

Beyond Triathlon

When the Guale Indians were all exhumed, they were taken to study for insights into their diet, nutrition, etc. The bones were taken with permission, and then reinterred in a special cemetery. We had a priest and Indian chief and placed a marker indicating that it was done appropriately and with permission. We tried to respect the Indians and tried to respect history. We sold the property and ended up building in Vermont on solid bedrock.

It was a wonderful opportunity to preserve some of our history and provide educational opportunities for children and the news media. But when the backhoe operator made the original discovery, it put a big monkey wrench in my training plans. Somehow, as well as training, working, and family responsibilities, I was now overseeing the archaeological professionals and volunteers. Plus, public relations people who seemed to have emerged from the shadows. Training and getting in workouts was always a challenge and I had to get better organized and use the obstacles presented, like it or not. So on some days this is what I did: I biked up to the Island, forty miles, I dug and screened for a few hours with the archaeologists, took a swim in the ocean and biked back to where my husband worked and he drove me home. I must admit, what he brought home—me—was much the worse for wear. My motto, "Soldier on!"

At the time, I was running a sports medicine clinic. I'd train in my lunch hour, train after work, go home, get dinner ready for the kids and then go back to work and set up all the records for the next day. But something went awry with my job there. I was given an evaluation for my employment there. I met with a woman and she looked like a humpty dumpty and obviously didn't know anything about health and nutrition.

She said, "You're doing a good job, but I have one complaint. Your hair is always wet."

I said, "Well, I do want to explain why my hair might be wet. I'm training for Ironman in Hawaii. In my lunch hour is when I swim. And sometimes I come back from swimming—and yes—my hair might be damp." It might not be wet, but it would be damp.

She said, "I'm sure you can correct that."

"No Ma'am," I said. And resigned.

Whenever I do reports on people I never bother with small stuff, just focus on the big things.

This episode affirms that the trails Dottie and Celeste followed were, at times, barely existent. As they pursued new personal goals, they pushed back overhanging foliage, stomped long grass down underfoot, and cleared a way through the forest. For Celeste, this meant persevering despite the expectations of those close to her, while for Dottie it meant refusing to allow the expectations of those who did not know her from progressing toward her goal.

Dottie decided to leave for Hawaii a few weeks early so that she could settle in and train without interruption from work, the dig and other activities. Like Celeste's story of the New York City Marathon, Dottie's account of her first attempt at an Ironman triathlon and the final weeks leading up to it differs from other sections of her memoir. It is more detailed and emotional. Intrigued by the account I decided that the idiosyncrasies that characterize her narrative should remain:

Arriving in Kona after a grueling flight one already is wondering, "What in ---- am I doing here?" The outdoor baggage claim creates anxiety by attacking us with relentless heat and a black lava landscape, which looks more than spooky.

This could be a really BIG mistake.

My mind is running wild: "What was I thinking to accept that letter? This is way beyond real. Did I train enough? How can an old lady like me ever finish? This is one bad nightmare!"

Once settled on "the Big Island," I start exploring and since I arrived three weeks before The Event the atmosphere is calm and quiet. Not for long. Each day sees more arrivals, more bikes, and more triathletes at restaurants.

On my first visit to "Dig Me" Beach all the beautiful, totally fit young ones are parading around in their micro-mini coverings or something resembling a very modified bathing suit. Now I feel positively fat after scanning this scene of lean bodies with no obvious body fat anywhere. When I look down the ocean, along the beach front, and am told, "That's where you swim to for the turnaround..." Well, I can't see that far and it already, in my mind's eye, seems at least one hundred miles away. I decide to go for a little run and calm down my severe nervous indigestion over the reality of the swim. After half a mile I am sweating buckets, panting hard, and knowing this is one BIG nightmare.

Finally, I met some of my own age groupers and we embrace in the knowledge that we are not alone. Several are experienced competitors and one woman, Louise Taylor, had won "Our" age group many times. (A total of eleven wins overall.) A local resident, Janet Olen, offers to take her kayak and accompany us on the swim course. Hallelujah!

The swim turned out to be manageable with our guide, Janet, and we even stopped frequently to observe the world beneath us. The brilliant tropical fish beneath us were unimaginable to me. I trained in the offshore murky Atlantic Ocean, which left to your imagination what might be down there, or New England lakes with mostly rocks, weeds and occasional drab colored life forms. We saw dolphins and schools of luminescent fish in blues, yellows and orange. The crystal clear ocean also revealed starkly defined black lava reefs where one never wanted to go. It was instant "bye bye," if you got swept there by the current.

Our routine became established and our early morning swims were followed by breakfast at a nearby restaurant. If our family members or other friends would join us, they would observe what we ate. My husband to this day says that he had "never seen such fit little (aging) ladies eat so much." The entire table was covered with dishes of pancakes, waffles, toast, juices, fruit, bacon, coffee, tea etc.

A run later each day took some preparation as we "planted" water bottles by roadside markers at least every five miles. Usually runs were twenty miles. Our markers were telephone poles or on the black lava fields, which had white stones for all types of graffiti and love messages, too. All of us had little idiosyncrasies for energy supplements or, sometimes, just comfort food. Janet would "plant" sweet potatoes.

Possibly the boost in confidence and morale that Dottie and other women garnered from this contact inspired Janet to invite women competitors aged forty and over to her home for a breakfast. This was the very first of the breakfasts Dottie and Celeste mentioned when we gathered at Celeste's home in Naples. As Dottie recounts, the resultant tradition highlighted the comfort and strength many of the masters women derived from the company of others like them. Dottie acknowledges the considerable variation in their backgrounds and experiences—the women came from all over the United States and beyond, and some journeys were exceptional. But wherever they came from it seemed that they all gained something from the breakfasts:

Each attendee would share a short talk about herself. The experiences were often emotional stories of the obstacles they overcame to come to this Ironman. One woman had breast cancer and trained when she was in remission, another mortgaged her home to pay for the trip, another came to dedicate her race to a dying mother, another was trying to recover from a recent divorce, and the list went on and on. Many of these women became our friends for life.

As Ironman progressed through the years, the Women's Masters Breakfast became a much honored and revered event. No matter the challenges to get to the race or the obstacles in the race there was the consolation and comfort of knowing we would all be together at "The Breakfast." It was always a relief, prior to the race, to be free of competition and expose the human side of our lives.

Surrounded by new friends, the terror induced by the thought of her upcoming attempt to conquer the epic distances and imposing setting of an event that was already the stuff of legends, appears to recede in Dottie's account:

Kona was a fun place to visit and we met many friendly shop and restaurant owners. We always went to Crazy Shirts to get souvenirs. Our friend, Crystal, owned ZOOT and worked out of her home and made bike shorts for us. Just look today and see how far her fledgling business has gone. From that small beginning it became a big corporation. The bike shop catered to our every need. Other Island residents became good friends. We biked around The Island with them and I got the nickname, "White Knuckles." The Island is loaded with mountains and narrow winding roads that are not biker friendly, thus my death grip on the handlebars. At one point in a ride I was talking to a fellow male triathlete and he just dropped off the side of the road down the mountainside. We patched him up with our first aid kit and went on. We did the Captain Cook Swim with friends, which was a safer adventure. It was an enjoyable time and distracted us from our anxieties about The Race. That apprehension was never far away.

A mandatory meeting was held before the race where the race director and many qualified staff related the rules of the race, especially no drafting. Doctors impressed upon us the importance of safety and proper preparation, prior to and on Race Day. "Hydration will make or break your race," we were told. You had to get weighed at certain points and if you lost too much weight you had to quit.

On the bike it was imperative to drink water or replacement fluid every eight minutes. Every five miles of the 112-mile bike course had an Aid Station. This was organized at the approach to each mile with a walkie talkie person who ran along side and took your order. A short way down was the fast food station with fluid, bananas, jelly sandwich (no more peanut butter), and anything else ordered. We could send a "Needs" bag to the half way mark at Hawi with anything we wanted or needed. I decided when I left home for The Race I would take frozen banana bread, which a friend had baked for me, and that would be my reward IF I ever got to that point.

While Dottie's narrative about her time at Kona oscillates between past and present tense a little, this tendency becomes more pronounced when she writes about "The Race" itself. She also shifts occasionally from first to second person. It feels like she is no longer telling a story with the reader in mind. She is re-living it through a collection of personal memories, like scenes in a film. They are embellished occasionally with observations from accumulated experience. But the specific memories still seem fresh and evocative, the emotion real:

The day before The Race the tension has reached its peak and "frenzy" describes all participants. At The King K. Hotel local volunteers are filling the lobby making real flower leis for Ironman finishers the next day. I only hope I get one! Clothes are turned in, special Needs delivered, and then bike inspection and racking.

Although I have done hundreds of races there is no other like Hawaii. After a sleepless night one starts advancing at 3:30 a.m. down pitch dark Alii Drive to the most unbelievable sight. It looks like a brightly lit carnival with thousands of bikes gleaming in hundreds of spotlights. Worker bees are everywhere connecting cables; T.V. trucks and booms dot the skyline; music blasts "Rocky," or "Wind Beneath My Wings," and banners are everywhere swinging in the breeze. We check in, get body marked and set up our bikes.

We feel naked without our sweats and towels and as we approach the swim we are shivering, chilled and scared. Goggles are a constant worry—leaking, getting knocked off, fogging up etc. I always pray before a race for the safety of all triathletes. Next thing we're waiting with wall-to-wall swimmers and I'm reminded of cattle herding through pens until you can get out. Finally, the gun goes off and we are OUT. (There are now wave starts to alleviate the congestion.) Once in the washing machine of thrashing swimmers, totally chaotic, it takes a while but I finally get into a rhythm. I swim a "Banana" Course, which means you start wide, not on the midline, and then cut in so the mass of swimmers has thinned out. It's never easy and every race is different. I swim over the rolling hills of the ocean like a roller coaster. Some were seasick. I was very surprised (shocked) when I saw scuba divers below me. Why didn't someone tell me? They were there to protect us if we had any difficulty. Well, they almost gave me difficulty. One concentrates on swimming but you can never let up because you need to meet the time limit and also pace well to try and accrue extra time so it can be added to the long and difficult bike course.

What a joy it is to get out of the swim and run through the showers, changing room, bike shorts, helmet and off on my bike. This is where my husband says, "It's like watching grass grow." He sees me for a few

6. A Giant Enchilada

At the start of the bike leg at the 1989 Bud Light Ironman Triathlon World Championship, Dottie is strong and determined (courtesy George Dorion).

moments and I'm off. "It's a long way to Tipperary," but now it's Hawi. Hours later, fighting a headwind, Hawi is in sight and my banana bread is there. I spy my friend Tina, from Canada, and we do a little dance and eat. This behavior, I understand, is unusual, maybe nutty, according to The Crew there. We figured if we got this far, halfway, we could surely get back. We did not have a big tailwind going back, that would be logical. But the wind didn't totally shift as it sometimes does, giving a headwind both ways.

George is there when I finish the bike, cheering me on. I quickly change to begin the run. He will now still be "watching Grass Grow" until midnight. We practice many hours to get our bike legs to turnover to run legs but it's tough. "Legs of Lead," I say and the "Marathon Shuffle" begins. You meet the nicest people "On the Road." Conversation keeps us going and it's walk, jog, walk, jog. Walk every mile marker through aid stations and get hot soup, fluid replacement, defizzed Coke, bananas although I pass up barbecue on the grill for another day. Each aid station has a contest to see which one is best and wins. Music, bright lights, and hula dancers can greet us. When you are really fatigued, the Hoyts go by with father pushing son in his wheelchair and that gives you an adrenalin rush and motivation to keep going. If they can do it surely we can! Onward. Finally there are lights in the distance. Every mile seems longer and longer but the lights are getting brighter, and brighter. I can hear music now. The crowds are cheering. Slog, slog, slog. The cramps are just beginning. Keep going.

Around the corner is The Finish and I hear the crowds cheering and the announcer naming the finishers. The final stretch is brightly lit with the crowds behind fences cheering and shouting. The Finish Line is in sight and I am in tears, and totally choked up. I cross! Valerie Silk, Race Director, puts a lei around my neck and says, "You are an Ironman." As I write this almost thirty years later, I am still in tears and am totally choked up.

However, all stories don't have a happy ending. While on the massage table after the Race I begin to vomit and experience extreme dizziness to faintness. I spent my celebration night/day in the hospital with I.V.'s and a diagnosis of hyponatremia and one of the lowest sodium and potassium levels of many years.

Told in wavering tense, and swinging between the collective and personal, Dottie almost seems to be distracted from the journey that her memoir narrates. She is enchanted with this clearing in the forest. Returning to it years later still evokes the magic and delight of discovery.

Less calculated than other parts of her memoir, the account sheds a different light on my original question: "What did Dottie set out to say?" What does she include when she is not trying to connect dots? What does she leave out? What looks different when she lingers on the freeze-framed memories of that "giant enchilada"?

Dottie's word choice tells me something. She has returned to the same dual theme of vulnerability and freedom that appears in the first chapter of her memoir. Originally, she labeled this chapter:

"'Free to Walk Around the Cabin' or in this case free to swim, bike and run around Kona, HI."

The former chapter title highlights the significance of the word— "free"—but the freedom to which Dottie gestures is complicated and subtle. It does not exist within itself; it is born out of vulnerability. The breakfast attendees were "free of competition," when they "expose[d] the human side of their lives."

In Dottie's account of the moment before race start, she and her peers again seem to be exposed. In that instance, feelings of vulnerability are evoked due to the absence of outer clothing. When Dottie describes the removal of sweatshirts and other clothing items that conceal the

Dottie looking fit and remarkably fresh after finishing the 1989 Bud Light Ironman Triathlon World Championship (courtesy George Dorion).

revealing skin suits underneath, she speaks in collective terms: "we feel naked." Were the masters women also free in that moment of physical vulnerability, perhaps because of that vulnerability?

Dottie often places quotation marks around terms that have specific meanings attached to them in the context of her story. Narrating her panic when she first arrived at Kona and her relief at finding masters women athletes, Dottie refers to "our" age group. But when she writes, "we feel naked," she does not place quotation marks around "we." Instead I find myself wanting to place quotation marks around the word. Why does Dottie use the collective "We" at this point? And why does she use it as if it is a given? She is not the only person rendered vulnerable as hundreds of ordinary people metamorphosed into honorary athletes, humbled before nature and the sporting excellence of the professional triathletes with whom they mingle.

But the "we" does not seem to allude to the accumulated mass of athletes awaiting the race start. It appears to point to the masters women with whom Dottie shared the interwoven sensations of vulnerability and freedom, the shared feeling that they were about to reach for a goal that no one else had set for them, to try something that no one expected from them. In the absence of the bondage of convention they are altogether ready and "free to swim, bike and run around Kona." It was a new freedom shared by a small group of women aged around forty and over. Dottie did not need to define the collective, because they had already exposed themselves to each other. While their stories differed, they were bound together by three things: gender, age, and their shared daring. Vulnerability and freedom meant something specific to the masters women who bobbed tentatively in the water awaiting the start of the 1985 Ironman World Championship.

7

Stepping Up

Dottie always enjoyed sport but running and triathlon opened a world of new possibilities for her. The same sports represented simply a means to an end for Celeste, a way of resisting the mold designed for her, of learning lessons about herself and life. She did not necessarily envisage herself as a perpetual athlete. Nor did she see herself as part of a collective when she reached the finish line at the 1986 Seafair Triathlon. Yet, like Dottie, Celeste took on many more multisport challenges following her initiation in the mid–1980s.

The coincidence of their mutual dabbling in triathlon with the structural consolidation of the sport meant that many opportunities enticed Dottie and Celeste to persist with their respective multisport adventures. The earliest version of a national triathlon governing body appeared in 1982. Tri-Fed, as it became known, secured an insurance agreement the following year and began to sanction events around the United States. The rules and objectives of the organization were drawn up in 1985, and annual memberships introduced in 1987.[1] During this period, races sprang up all over the country. Some originated under the aegis of the commercial U.S. Triathlon Series (USTS) first run by Jim Curl and Carl Thomas in 1982 and sponsored by Bud Light for a few years from 1984. From 1985 Tri-Fed recognized some USTS events and other independent triathlons as qualifying races for the national championships.[2] In the late 1980s, the Ironman brand expanded into an international series of ultra-distance events, while a number of preliminary efforts to establish an international federation led to the foundation of the International Triathlon Union in 1989. Dottie and Celeste in effect transformed into triathletes at the same time that triathlon transformed into a sport.

---

1. USA Triathlon, "Timeline," USA Triathlon History Project, last modified 2020, https://www.teamusa.org/USA-Triathlon/About/Multisport/History.

2. Jim Curl, "The U.S. Triathlon Series (USTS) History: 1982–1993," USA Triathlon History Project, last modified 2020, https://www.teamusa.org/USA-Triathlon/About/Multisport/.

Beyond Triathlon

Over the ensuing two decades or so Dottie and Celeste each competed in 250 odd triathlons and other events. In their original memoirs, they compress the process of training for and competing in them into bridging sentences and montages of honorable mentions. As they guide their readers along their respective paths, they mark out divergent trails through the forest of personal significance, but they do not describe every tree or wildflower, every waterfall or fern. Both trails head in the same direction—up. Leaving the valley behind, they seem driven to reach new vantage points from which to survey the landscape. Dottie traverses back and forth, describing the view here and there, while Celeste pushes toward and scales straight up the sheer, relentless rock face of athletic endeavor.

For Celeste, Kona is just a small detail in another story that began at the Seafair Triathlon two days before she moved to Denver. Although she had no aim other than completion of the event, something that happened minutes after "the End" gave Celeste reason to continue on her journey into the athletic unknown:

And then we gathered for the awards.

Our club sat on the grass on a steep hillside with all the others, a table of trophies and medals way down below. In those days there were no five-year age groups. It was the first five younger than thirty-five, first five older. They called first the five leading men and then the five leading women in the categories Under 35. Then they did the Over 35. I still had no concept of time or placement. I just knew my age. Forty-three. I heard third place called out and a woman in front of me excitedly waddled up off the grass to head down below. I was puzzled. "I beat her," I said to the person next to me. Then it began, very slowly, to dawn. They were doing five, four, three ... number two was called. It was not me. And then I knew.

I began to laugh uncontrollably.

"And in first place, from Mercer Island, Celeste Callahan."

This moment was one of my life's best. I would count this moment as one of life's happiest, along with seeing my first child for the first time.

Later that day, Dick called from Denver. "How was the triathlon?" he asked.

"I won," I said.

The next day, flowers. And the day after that, the unknown. Or the known: Square One.

Celeste may have been initiated in Seattle, but her second athletic metamorphosis—this time into a triathlete—took place primarily while living in Denver. As with the marathon journey, she takes the time to work through that process in her memoir, embellishing it with humor and emotion, and scattering more clues as to the final destination of the memoir.

Except that it wasn't Square One. I won a plane ticket at the race in Seattle. I used it to go back to the Washington State Triathlon Championships in September. Several things happened when I did. I began to bond with a group that had panache for me, who always turned down teas that featured cooking equipment or lingerie.

What I liked; I had all these friends who saw me as me. I got seen as me for the first time at the Washington Park bathroom when someone came and approached me for me. It's as though you're naked and someone sees through you.

There it is again—the word "naked." In this case, Celeste skips the part where exposure gives rise to feelings of vulnerability. She relishes the lack of convention and expectation, her metaphorical nakedness. For both Celeste and Dottie, triathlon appears to strip away convention.

Caroline had let me stay at her house; she was out of town. So I visited some friends, and I ate my dinner. I remember now with whom: Linda. I was in my forties and she must have been twenty years younger. She was the first adult person that I recall thinking was *cool.* She had obviously dyed blond hair that had been over-permed or was naturally curly and unkempt. I was so envious. I remember the Pachelbel Canon played on the restaurant music thing. I remember that it reminded me of the Mary Tyler Moore film in which her older son had killed himself. I remember being on a big adventure. I was doing a triathlon away, away from home, winning a plane ticket at the Seattle Seafair two months before and since then moving to Denver.

I remember going to bed at eight when it was still light outside. I remember not sleeping a wink. I remember the rain in the morning and how we could hardly see across the water for the swim. There were no boats out the way we have them now. The swimmers—I do not remember there being wave starts—just went. There was a strobe light at the turn around, and my nemesis, Joyce, wore a half wetsuit. No one wore wetsuits then and Seattle water was frigid—sixty something degrees. The bike was OK, but I was told later than my jacket, unzipped, was blowing in the wind and probably caused drag, something else I did not know about. Then came the run. I flew.

The party after the awards was fun. I got sixth place. It made no difference to me except that I had won the last one, which Joyce did not do. Joyce's husband was very kind. Dick. He told me what I had to do to make it to the podium next time. It was my bike holding me back. I am going to guess it was a twenty-five-mile bike because it was a 10K run. (I cannot imagine having swum a mile.) Maybe I did. In those days the distances were uneven and different each time; one signed up for an event and just did it. So I am thinking that my bike ride may have been two hours. He told me that, to improve, I had to ride hills of 6 percent grade, a concept foreign to me. He said that I needed to take off at least a half hour from my bike time.

The biggest thing in triathlon in the 80s was the Bud Light Series. It was the only thing in triathlon. For my next race, Caroline asked me to go with her to Chicago to do a Bud Light.

I said, "Why would I do that?"

She said: "IT IS BUD LIGHT."

I did not get it. But all I had to do to qualify for the national championships at Hilton Head in 1987 was get in the top ten of my age group in the Bud Light Series, which turned out to be easy because in the women's 40–44 age group there were usually less than ten there.

Training back in Denver one day, I stopped to do an errand on my bike. The shop owner told me to talk to the fellow in the back, that he was a triathlete too. Fellow told me about a masters swim group one mile from our new house. And a triathlon club. So I joined a proper triathlon club, with men and women of all ages—but mostly white men. There was not a lot of diversity in that part of town.

Wanting to be with my Seattle friends who were training for the national championships at Hilton Head the following year, I asked the swim coach to personally guide me toward that goal, the journey to which I could not fathom. He asked what I paid in Seattle for the club coach. I told him $18 a month. I still feel guilty.

I had to learn from scratch. One plus one plus one does not make three. With triathlon you are using different muscles. It is intellectually stimulating. Each discipline is different from the next. Each one has its own clothing, equipment and jargon.

I had to get a bike made for me. My coach said I had to ride a hundred miles a week. When I rode with the club, I was the weakest link. It's my best sport now because I spent a lot of time at it. I spent a lot of time on my bike alone. It was fun. My husband asked me what I thought about all those hours. I was pretending that I was a star. Or I wrote speeches in my head. Or I imagined greatness. My favorite ride is from home in Central Denver to Evergreen up Bear Creek Canyon. I then used to turn around three miles down the road at Kittredge to make the trip an even fifty miles. It took me four hours. I felt so delivered as I would sit in the tub. My sins, my imperfections had been wiped clean.

The next spring, I went back to Seattle to see friends. The woman who at that time was the hot-shot masters triathlete asked me to go biking. I beat her up all the hills and she did not turn up for the two races that I showed up to do in that city.

My coach, Dave, helped me and I did four of the USTS Bud Light races.

The 1987 Bud Light USTS included races at Houston and Phoenix.

Houston was an interesting beginning. Dave wanted to watch me and drove from Denver all the way there. I was kind of embarrassed because I had invited my sister to go and be with me. It looked a little shady to have this errant man on the premises. He camped out and we stayed in something Kathleen called the Beirut Hilton. Triathlon lodging is of another culture. "Aids-a-Rama," my friend Heidi used to say.

I remember going to dinner the night before the race. I asked Dave if I should have a beer. He said, whatever relaxes you. We then went to the pre-race meeting, which scared the tuna salad out of me, making me realize that that was exactly what all pre-race meetings were going to

An apprehensive Celeste about to don her wetsuit for the Panama City Beach Triathlon in the 1980s (courtesy Kathleen Haik).

do. All the, "DO THIS DO NOT DO THAT." It was like St. Paul to the Corinthians.

The next morning Dave was to come meet us for pancakes, but he did not come. So we went by ourselves, a gutsy thing as far as I was concerned. I had actually made a decision. It turns out that it had rained the night before, and Dave had spent the dawn picking his gear out of the mud. I now wish I had gotten him his own room. I am sure it was about $49.

We drove to the race and I set up, meeting a friend from Seattle who remarked that, unlike her, I had on makeup. So much to learn. I learned a lot that morning, like "never ever separate yourself from your swim cap." Do not trust anyone to hold it while you go to the bathroom. Dave had wandered off talking to people and I had to tell the man with the megaphone, and I got another.

People will try to psyche you out. One woman in my age group saw my age on my leg and I said, "Hi, where are you from?"

She looked at me and sneered, "From altitude. New Mexico. Where are YOU from?"

"Colorado," I answered and walked off.

During the race I learned, "improve your swim stroke" and "do not change into bike shorts when you are wet."

My bike time was 1 hour and 15 minutes. But the run was killer humidity. I learned then to study the temperatures in which I would compete.

I also lost a diamond out of a ring I had. Why I remember that now, I do not know.

I finished second at Phoenix and in the top five for the series. So Dave got me to nationals in Hilton Head in 1987. Just as I got out of the car at Stapleton Airport, Dave leaned over and said: "There are no excuses, Celeste. Just remember that." That one became bronzed into my central nervous system. I think I owe who I have become to that one. When Dick and I played tennis, and I told him of a malady, he would say: "You are just making up a reason to lose." It took me to the nationals to know what he meant.

There ARE no excuses.

There was a storm the night before the nationals and you had to walk a mile to the swim start. No excuses.

Hilton Head had a huge screen. Afterwards, when it showed "Women 45–49, 5th place Celeste Callahan," you could hear, "Oh my!" I finished top five at the best, most flamboyant nationals in the history of the sport, and I turned in my best time— EVER—in my largest age group EVER.

Unlike the account of her second attempt at the Seafair Triathlon, Celeste chooses not to narrate any details about her experience of the swim, cycle or run at the 1987 USA National Triathlon Championships at Hilton Head. The focus on training, on lessons learned, and the competitiveness apparent in the remembered exchanges with other women in Celeste's account of her journey to the nationals, suggests a stronger focus on improvement rather than on completion. Celeste had already committed to the trail into the forest of multisport and seems fixated on its offshoot, the steep path to the top of the age group rankings. Instead of narrating the race itself, Celeste's memoir reflects on the journey that led to a top five finish in the 45–49 age group at the 1987 national championships.

USTS HILTON HEAD
September 27, 1987
Marathon Foto

Celeste is focused as she heads into transition after the swim leg at the 1987 Hilton Head National Triathlon Championships (courtesy Marathon Foto).

It seemed that the beginnings did not end. We would reach one level, as a toddler climbs the stairs, and see another—another beginning that took us into territory yet unexplored. My first triathlon led to another after a year in serious training—I likened that to the unreachable goal of the New York Marathon. The plane ticket back to the Washington State Championships was another stair step. I took the gauntlet as I saw what work was required to dispatch with a decent race. I got a

 **USTS HILTON HEAD**
September 27, 1987
Marathon Foto

Celeste celebrates as she finishes the 1987 Hilton Head National Triathlon Championships. Fitness, preparation and focus resulted in her fastest Olympic distance triathlon time and a top five age group placing (courtesy Marathon Foto).

coach to help me get to nationals. I trained. Sometime before nationals I remember talking to a woman from Seattle who said, "I just want to finish 2 hours and 30 minutes." I got fifth at nationals out of forty, my best ever against so many, and I finished with my best time to date of 2 hours and 32 minutes.

I thought, well, maybe I AM good.

While Celeste alludes to new athletic goals as "steps," not all of her athletic goals elicited profound revelations. The "steps" or new beginnings highlighted in her memoir, were tied to the acquisition of new knowledge about herself and the unleashing of previously unrecognized personal potential. Completion of the New York City Marathon led to the revelation that men progress in the world because they learn through sport to strive for goals that are "slightly over their heads." Celeste strived to qualify for 1987 nationals. She reached her goal and discovered that she possessed greater athletic capacity than she imagined. She did not finish quite as close to the top of the age group rankings at the Wilkes Barre national championships the following year, but success in 1987 fueled greater confidence and independence in 1988:

I went all by myself to race nationals in Wilkes Barre. It was an experience to get off the plane, get a rental car, wait for my bike and luggage, find the motel, find a bike shop to help me put together my bike, find the course and drive and ride it.

I was so confident. But at that race where it rained cats and dogs, I finished tenth.

Toward the end of the 1988 triathlon season, Celeste competed in the Ironman World Championships at Hawaii for the first time. It does not seem that Celeste planned to qualify for the event, but it was another goal on which to set her sights, once the opportunity arose. It was a step up in distance, but, like the 1988 nationals and the Mount Rainier climb, not a personal step up. It did not lead to a new perspective, to a new outlook from a higher vantage point along the multisport trail. In contrast to Dottie's emotional stream-of-consciousness recollection, Celeste writes nothing in her memoir about her debut Ironman triathlon, suggesting that it was not a transformative experience as such. When prodded, Celeste furnished the following:

I qualified at Utah on July 4. It was the Independence Day Triathlon, probably a one off. I didn't know that it was a qualifier. It was a quarter of the Ironman distance. They didn't tell me straight away. I finished fifth and they had to see who else wanted the Ironman spot. The Ironman organizers called someone else and she didn't want it, so they called me.

Ironman was around the same time as our twentieth anniversary, in October 1988. I said to Dick, "I know where we can go for our anniversary—Hawaii."

I had only trained for shorter triathlons, and only had until October to triple my distances. I remember swimming. I rode my bike, just got on it and rode as much as I could and left home at 5 a.m. for an eighteen-mile run, getting back for the 8 a.m. carpool.

I practiced in my head that when the gun went off, I was going to smile. I was concerned how I would feel in the Pacific Ocean. When training for Ironman we went to Monaco for a business trip. I swam thirty minutes in the ocean and got sick in my stomach. The first time I swam at Hawaii, I spent thirty minutes swimming and again got sick and spent forty minutes throwing up.

A doctor gave me a Scopolamine patch to put behind the ear for motion sickness. It took away the taste of the water, and I was fine. I was able to do the Ironman. Riding the bike, I was thinking, "I'm in the Ironman." The little one (my youngest son) wanted to come. He was so excited: "Mom was running in Ironman!"

But that was that. I didn't have a spectacular ending. I got my first lei from race director Valerie Silk, which is a big thing to say. I just saw her and said hello.

Hawaii was exciting but not that exciting for me.

Learning about their metamorphosis into runners, I hypothesized that Celeste appears to draw satisfaction and validation from recognition by men, Dottie from evidence of her improving capacity as an athlete. As she makes a second metamorphosis into triathlete, Celeste displays greater consciousness of times and rankings. But she still enjoys a nod of the head from significant male others:

One time, the Australian woman who shared carpool with us asked Colin where his mother shopped or went to the cleaners or the hair salon. When she asked what I did for exercise, he at thirteen said, "You don't want to know."

After my first Ironman, my parents were visited by a friend, who came to tell them that her daughter had just done the N.Y.C. Marathon. My dad said, "We listened very politely and then ... we shot her down in flames." That was probably the greatest compliment he ever gave me.

But at the conclusion of the 1988 Ironman World Championship, Celeste had not completely metamorphosed into a triathlete. She saw no future for herself in the sport. She had pursued some novel athletic goals. Some of them led to personal revelations and growth. Some did not.

7. Stepping Up

Triathlon still seemed as remote from normality as the volcanic slopes of Hawaii's Big Island were from the Rocky Mountains of Colorado. In her account, Celeste offers a key reason for persisting with the multisport adventure:

I planned that Ironman would be my last race. I had taken enough family time and money. Then the kids gave me aero bars for Christmas, and I remember saying, incredulous: "You mean, I can continue?"

Invented in the 1980s, aero bars attach to the handlebar of a bike and extend forward, with padded forearm rests, allowing riders to drop their upper body down and reduce wind resistance. Gifted with the latest in triathlon equipment, Celeste felt like she had the approval of her family. She lined up at Kona again in 1989 and set her sights again on the national championships. They were not significant goals in themselves. Yet, combined, they signal that she had "stepped up." Celeste's second metaphorical metamorphosis was complete. Triathlon, like running, was no longer a deviation from a pre-ordained path. Triathlon had become something that Celeste did, something other than the role she long believed to be her prime purpose in life; being the wife of a successful man and mother.

Nationals was always a priority on my schedule. At the University of Nebraska, among the Sigma Chis, I had long been, till recently, an enigma. "Who was the girl who got Dick Callahan?" was how they put it. I could never go with him, a former Big Shot McGuire in the '60s, because Fall was the time for nationals and worlds. Even in these enlightened times, no one had a wife who had her own athletic achievements and a plan to be elsewhere instead of watching college football.

I think once we had words.

Celeste completed her debut Ironman triathlon in 1988. By that stage, Dottie had already returned to Hawaii for a second attempt at the ultradistance event. As with Celeste's second national championships, Dottie's second Ironman triathlon does not appear as a personal "step up." In contrast to the emotional tone of the account of her first, Dottie resumes her focus on athletic performance in narratives of her subsequent attempts. In 1987, misfortune confounded her competitive aims:

You never know what's going to happen in an Ironman. I was on my way to the home stretch of the bike course and setting an age-group record for the cycling portion. That thought was immediately interrupted by "thump, thump, thump." No one ever wants to hear the disastrous warning of a flat tire. I undid my spare tire pack under my saddle and proceeded to change the tire and inflate it with my CO2 cartridge.

Off I went with a sigh of relief. About five minutes later I once again heard, "thump, thump, thump." It couldn't be true, but it was. I stood by my disabled bike and was shouting and crying and my language was not ladylike. The volunteers assured me that the emergency repair truck was coming, and it did. (Originally, we had no support services or mechanics) They changed another tire and I was on my way, minus any record. As the famous saying goes, "The best made plans of mice and men often go awry." This time I would say, "The best made plans of Ironman participants often go to ----."

Dottie finished sixth in her age group in 1985 but dropped to seventh in 1987. She returned to Hawaii in 1989, the same year as Celeste's second attempt, with hopes for a better result and justified her efforts by finishing fourth in her age group with a personal best time.

But competitive goals alone do not explain Dottie's continued participation in multisport and other athletic challenges. Nor is her persistence explained by a desire to continuously "step up." Rather it appears to have been tied to a growing perception of herself as a triathlete. Like Celeste, this personal "step up" seems to have occurred with assurances of approval or interest on the part of her family. Occasionally Dottie involved family members in her triathlon journey:

A most memorable Ironman in Florida was a relay with our two sons and George cheering us on. I did the swim, second son Tim did the bike and Mark, eldest son, did the run. Mark, our ultramarathoner, became sick during the run and yet persisted to finish in the dark of night. Still, it was very special to have shared this experience with adult children.

The early triathlon experiences narrated by Dottie and Celeste diverge markedly in focus and tone, demonstrating that no single event is guaranteed to produce common feelings of empowerment, freedom, or self-confidence in its female competitors. Reflecting on them I wonder once more about where their stories intersect, and about the over-riding point that Dottie and Celeste are trying to make. Whether intended or not, have they provided hints as to where these accounts of assorted multisport adventures are leading?

I return to the points where the respective stories of metamorphosis seem to converge. Both achieved self-designated athletic goals, but not before experiencing feelings of vulnerability. Dottie details a crisis in confidence with physical manifestations when confronted by the reality of Ironman triathlon in 1985, particularly the swim. Celeste describes the physical experience of panic when she recounts her decision

Just a fraction of the running and multisport events in which Dottie participated in the 1980s and '90s are represented in this patchwork quilt of race finisher tee shirts (courtesy Jane E. Hunt).

to enroll in her very first triathlon at Seattle in 1984. Both acknowledge that the approval of family members contributed to some extent to their persistence. As Dottie and Celeste describe their continued exploration of the new landscape into which they have ventured, their memoir accounts evoke a growing sense of confidence in their ability to navigate its unknown obstacles. In Dottie's account references to nakedness disappear, while Celeste uses the term to connote personal freedom. Yet I still cannot see where athletic liberty is leading them. And us.

One thing is clear. Having metamorphosed into versions of themselves that counted triathlon as something that they did, rather than an end in itself, both Dottie and Celeste continued to "step up" athletically, although they make only fleeting reference to many of their new adventures. As a researcher interested in the links between sport and personal development in masters women athletes, these passing gestures to major achievements are intriguing. Why do Dottie and Celeste feel no need to elaborate on them in their memoirs, yet place enough weight on them to rescue them from the silence of history altogether? At the risk of diverting from the paths that Dottie and Celeste are forging through their memoir narratives, I decided to investigate the trails they mark with a cross.

Some events represented a twist on the by then established triathlon formula of swim, bike and run. Among them, the 1993 S.O.S. Survival of the Shawangunks, stands out in Dottie's memory:

I'd like to talk about SOS, hosted by the Mohonk Mountain House, in New York. I was the oldest woman to do it, and there was a sweeper behind me. I had a coach who got me into this—it was a limited numbers race. There were time limits for each leg. I was proud of being the last participant—I made the cut off. I was almost disqualified, but because they had waves, the last wave had extra time.

It was Survival definitely. I think it was one of the most challenging triathlons, more challenging than Ironman.

This is quite a statement, given that the accumulated distance of the SOS fell short of the Ironman equivalent, but Dottie's account reveals that the challenge lay not in the distance so much as in the conditions and the terrain that characterized the event.

It was a very hard race and the water was freezing and the only way out was on a stretcher. First, we biked thirty miles, then ran four miles on forest trails and then we swam 1.1 miles in the first freezing cold lake. Then we ran 5.5 miles then swam 0.4 miles in another freezing cold lake, and then we ran another eight miles, and then we swam the 0.5 miles into a beautiful resort with lots of people clapping and cheering. But that was not it. We had to then run up a steep climb to a monument. It was a very long, a very hard day.

The water was so cold it was warmer to swim around the edge, even though it was longer. But there were twigs etcetera around the edge. It put me in a crazy situation where I had to decide how I was going to swim it.

I was very smart about one thing. People swam with pants, etcetera, on. I decided to get a waterproof water pack and put my shoes in there. Before I swam, I would take my shoes off and put them in there. It was like a bubble on my back, like a pull buoy. So I had an advantage. It kept me swimming up high.

It was so pristine and beautiful. We ran around the Gunks, which are the big climbing mountains in the area. It was the most beautiful day and I had the most beautiful views. I was taking it all in. Every race you do you just remember something. This was the day I had the most spectacular weather. It was absolutely magnificent, and the people were wonderful and the people behind me, they were so nice.

Returning to the hotel after the final run leg, I passed a little old lady. In a thick New York City accent she said, "Oh my gawd. Look at that lady and her legs. Just look at those legs. How did she do that race? Oh my gawd, and she's not so young." This was a compliment to me because my husband picked me out of a photograph, before we met, because he liked my legs.

It was really a great event with a big celebration afterwards and for the first time I was really proud that I even finished it.

If my coach told me I had to finish running up a steep, steep climb, I probably wouldn't have done it. But it's one that I will always remember.

In the case of the SOS, the natural environment added to both the challenge and the reward for Dottie, but participation in the event appears to matter for other reasons. Dottie emphasizes the tenuousness of her continued participation in the arduous race, the persistent risk of being forced out. It feels as if the struggle is almost a metaphorical one for inclusion. The struggle for inclusion relates not just to gender, but to age; after all Dottie begins the account by stating that she was the "oldest woman."

Age appears to contribute to pride as Dottie narrates other events from the late 1980s and the 1990s as well. Not only did she step up by participating in at least one challenging off-road multisport event, Dottie also extended on her newly acquired abilities as a swimmer. For Dottie, swimming initially presented the most difficult aspect of triathlon. She devoted considerable attention to her aquatic deficiencies, making it possible to participate in Ironman triathlons and SOS, and to collect the sort of memories that such multisport ordeals supplied.

It also provided her with the opportunity to engage in a whole new field of sporting endeavor. Among the obligatory mentions that comprise Dottie's montage of sporting achievements, are the 1988 FINA Masters World Swimming Championships and the 1997 Swim Around Key West. Her memoir barely mentions the former, although Dottie notes briefly that she threw discus and javelin in the 1980 Masters World Track and Field Championships at Puerto Rico, re-visiting a skill her father taught her as a child:

Our neighborhood has never been the same. I practiced running down our road holding the javelin high, looking like a spear, and running to our empty lot and throwing

Dottie decided to go for a swim in the freezing cold ocean while holidaying in New Zealand in 1994 (courtesy George Dorion).

it as hard as I could to the lake. I never had a traffic problem with my "spear."

When prompted during a conversation at her Jacksonville home, Dottie volunteered no details about the 1988 Masters World Swimming Championships. A cutting found in her private collection, with no clues to its origin, explains that she qualified for, but missed, the 1986 Ironman triathlon due to a serious cycling accident. While recovering she concentrated on her swimming and established a masters swim club to address a lack of suitable instruction for middle aged and older athletes in Jacksonville. A local philanthropist sponsored members of the club to participate in the championships, held in Brisbane, Australia. Though pleased to qualify Dottie says nothing about the experience itself in her memoir. Instead she notes briefly the success of the American team, and the foundation of a program called "Every Child a Swimmer" as a legacy of the

The strength and confidence Dottie gained through her focused swim training shows in this photograph as she finishes the swim leg of a USTS event in the 1980s (Dottie Dorion Collection).

trip. The scheme enabled 12,000 children to have swimming lessons in three years.

Dottie says only a little in her memoir about the 1997 Swim Around Key West, but she does at least write about the personal experience: it was spectacular, she swam in a three-woman team, and they beat the men's team. She said enough to prompt me to ask about it. Unlike the 1988 masters, Dottie readily elaborated on an endeavor that probably would have required some courage to undertake, particularly for a woman of over sixty years of age:

In 1997 we had a wonderful Masters Swim program in states and cities and towns. And we decided we should do a relay race around Key West and we got a team of three women together. It included a naval officer who was a former competitive swimmer, and a young woman who was a ranked swimmer (tall, thin and looking like a trapezoid), in addition to me. The Masters group also got a men's team together and we decided to have a little competition against them. We were organized. We had a boat, a captain, and a map. The guys were not very organized.

They got their own boat and didn't have supplies. We helped them out a bit.

The total distance was a little over twelve miles, each team member swimming approximately four miles. When the day came, I had the first leg because they thought it would be easiest. I started OK because we had a small current. Then we turned the corner and there were cruise ships. One had a motor going, like a washing machine. And I saw an ugly fish, with ugly crooked teeth—a barracuda. It was awful, although I never heard of it attacking anyone. The navy swimmer took the next leg and there was a great current. She could barely turn her arms over quickly enough.

The last leg was harder. We noticed the men's boat going off course. We tried to wave to them but didn't try too hard. We took a little bit of a lead, but they came back as the swim course turned for the shore, and we were even. I had bet them all these things, and they were trying to negotiate with us. Both of the final swimmers took off, neck and neck, but the women won by seconds.

We never heard the end of it, because the newspaper got hold of it and I had fun running with it. It just pays to put in a little planning. I've learned from experience, get the best path and the best route.

This anecdote demonstrates the extent of Dottie's improvement as a swimmer, as well as her daring, and the satisfaction she derived from completing the challenge. Reflecting on her willingness to elaborate on the 1997 Swim but not the 1988 Masters, it seems to me that the Swim Around Key West represented more of a personal challenge to Dottie; a greater step up.

Celeste's athletic endeavors diversified and multiplied from the late 1980s as well. Like Dottie, most of the events in which Celeste participated disappear into the blurred landscape of her memoir narrative. It seems that, in terms of what she wants to say, the reader only needs to know that she continued to step up. It is clear that I, the curious historian, am more interested than Celeste and Dottie in the stories behind all of their new race medals. Likewise, I am interested in an aspect of Celeste's non-athletic life that she chose not to document in the memoir. During a conversation at her home in Florida I ask Celeste to tell me about key developments that took place in the mid–1990s. She complied.

In 1993, her life was disrupted once more by Dick's ever-progressing career. It entailed relocation, not to another part of the United States, but to London. Celeste's response to the move demonstrates the extent of her personal transformation.

7. Stepping Up

We were in London from 1993 to 1996. My husband was head of U.S. cellular. He was at the ground floor of US West Cellular, and then they made it international.

Right after we moved, within the first week, my husband had a dinner engagement with an ambassador, or someone who didn't mean anything to me. He didn't speak to me. I said I wanted to go home. And when Dick came home, he said that the ambassador was impressed because no one ever walked out on him before.

I said, "I've got to get to a swimming pool. I've got to do something. That's part of my lifestyle." He agreed. I then found a place to swim at Swiss Cottage, a station up the Tube. At the pool I heard someone ahead of me say, "I'm going to the Masters Swim squad," so I said the same thing. I did it three times a week. It was a source of great strength to me. I did a lot of swim meets, one on the Isle of Wight.

Running was easy. Right after we'd gotten there, I heard about a running race at Hyde Park, so I turned up. It turns out I knew the head of British Triathlon. He was there. There was a 5K or 10K and I was the first woman to finish. It was good.

The next thing to do was drive my car. I got my driver's license. I failed my first test. And I hit a truck with the Mercedes. Then I got a Volkswagen and put my bike in the back. Twice a week I'd drive out of town and ride a lot. We were burgled in the first month. They took all my gold jewelry and the first thing I did was check my bikes.

I joined the British Triathlon Union and I'd go to their races.

I had a busy enough life. There was a couple I met through triathlon before we moved to London, Gordon and Jackie, and they became good friends as well. It was enjoyable.

I did the London marathon twice. London is harder. You're running on cobble stones past the Tower of London. I loved it but it seemed harder. By that time, I thought I could run faster so I felt competitive. It finished in front of a palace. It was different. You're doing a hometown thing. Your neighbors know. New York is a destination. I noticed the crowds in New York. In the part where you go over the bridge to the Bronx there's silence. And when the sound picks up again it's amazing. The wall of sound cannot be believed. It's never quiet. London doesn't have that.

We'd also go back in summertime to the States and I'd race there. I did the duathlon national championships in 1993, because I could run. I did that in Atlanta. It was so casual. I didn't stay for the awards, but I qualified for the 1994 Duathlon World Championships in Hobart,

Australia. I was packed and ready to go to the Worlds and found out on the Wednesday before that I had cancer.

In London, my parents had been visiting and I hadn't had a period for a while. My mother said that I needed to go to the doctor. After they left I did, then I went to hospital and had a biopsy. The next night, I ran three seven-minute miles. After the last one I had blood running down my legs. The doctor said, "Tuesday you will have results." On Wednesday I called and was told to go and see him at 2 p.m. that afternoon. After he gave me the news, I was told "you can go to the race or not." I decided not to go to Hobart. But I asked the doctor if I could run the London marathon in four months. He said, "No woman has asked me that. Most women ask if they can drive." Two weeks later I went swimming. And I just ran the London marathon that year, not very well because I didn't have a womb.

Celeste's memoir is silent about the move to London and her brush with cancer. Her reaction to both hurdles certainly affirms the completion of her transformation into an athlete. Athletic goals gave her direction, as well as some form of continuity. She readily found a place within the triathlon community of her new homeland. But I wonder whether Celeste's silence is a sign that the personal obstacles did not prompt another personal "step up." With her return to full health, Celeste undertook more novel or extreme athletic challenges, much like Dottie. She took the time to mention them in her memoir, although they, too, do not seem to be transformative experiences.

In 1999 I read about Ironman Israel in the paper. The Israeli Army ran it. Dick and I went for two weeks, but it was Christmas and I didn't want my husband with me while I was doing a triathlon. He went home. So it was me and two pro's [*professionals*] and a guy who owned a kibutz. He was so afraid I'd beat him, so I let him go by. Going home, there was a big hold up at the airport, because they asked me, "Why isn't your husband with you?"

Not all of Celeste's post-cancer athletic challenges involved swimming, cycling and running:

Earlier, I had a friend call me in London and said she heard about the Race Across America. She said there was some sort of meet up on the web, and two women were looking to Ride Across America. I was recovering from cancer and by that time I was starving to ride.

The Race Across America (RAAM) is a 3,000-mile cycling race that traverses the United States from Oceanside, California to Annapolis, Maryland in a single stage. Amateurs and professionals compete as solo

Celeste and Colin waiting in Utah at the start of the next leg of the Ride Across America in 2008, when she participated in RAAM for a third time (courtesy Sam Wilcox).

riders or in teams of two, four or eight.[3] For a woman who, a decade earlier rode the bike leg of a short distance triathlon with a quarter in her shoe, RAAM represented a significant "step up" athletically. Still living in London, Celeste trained by riding to Cambridge and back.

The idea of riding across America might have had some appeal, but Celeste says little about it in her memoir. When asked, Celeste explained that the race was a logistical nightmare:

The only thing was that we had to pay $35,000—the estimated cost for food, water, running an RV, and two cars. One car was to follow a rider and another one leapfrog to take the next rider up to the next spot while the others would rest. My son said he would help with the crew. So there were three 19 year olds and they took over.

The whole thing was ghastly. It was hard, hard work. When we got

---

3. Race Across America, 2020, https://www.raceacrossamerica.org/.

Celeste and Colin may have lain down on the road in jest during the 2008 Ride Across America, but there is no doubt that the event was exhausting for athletes and their support crews (courtesy Sam Wilcox).

to sleep the first night in the hotel, I was in the same room as Colin's classmate. Another time I got a phone call in the middle of the night from my son and he said, "Mom, I can't find the R.V."

We were the second to last finishers. But we were the first team of women to do it.

It seems extraordinary to me that Celeste says nothing about the athletic experience of riding three thousand miles. I see it as another sign, like her silence about cancer, or Dottie's fleeting reference to the Swim Around Key West. The narrative blocks, like navigation crosses in a running event, tell the reader that those trails do not lead to the finish line. Instead, when I ask Dottie and Celeste about those trails, they re-direct my attention. Concluding her brief discussion of RAAM, Celeste notes that she was part of the first team of women to complete the event. Dottie mentions participating in masters events, or in masters swim teams, and the pride that she felt as an older woman finishing the epic SOS.

The message seems to be that the memoirs are not meant to be auto-biographical. Race medals and life stories are not the point of the project.

The continuous cycle of riding and re-grouping in hotel rooms crowded with equipment led to interesting dining arrangements (courtesy Sam Wilcox).

The memoirs do not catalogue sporting achievements and personal hurdles. They are about the new lives to which Dottie and Celeste gained access as a result of continuously "stepping up." The individual steps were small, but the accumulated progress resulted in personal transformation. The memoirs have more to do with becoming and being masters women triathletes.

8

Masters in Motion

As Dottie and Celeste narrate their travels through the athletic wilderness, I catch glimpses of other women forging their way through the same new landscape—women who, like them, grew to adulthood before the passing of Title IX. Celeste says quite a lot about Jan when she recounts her metamorphosis into a runner in South Dakota. Dottie and Celeste both allude to other masters women competitors at Ironman and other triathlons. Like Dottie and Celeste, the adventurers that flash in and out of their memoirs are doggedly carving their own way through the undergrowth, determined to reach a self-designated landmark on the horizon. The race results for the 1989 Bud Light Ironman Triathlon World Championship reveal that women aged forty and over represented less than seven percent of the field at the race start. Only one of them did not finish, while eleven younger women and more than forty men of various ages failed to cross the finish line.[1]

The memoirs introduce the reader to some of these explorers and flag their importance to the stories that Dottie and Celeste have to tell. But neither narrator introduces the other or mentions just where or when they met. Anecdotally Celeste acknowledged some awareness of Dottie in the late 1980s:

I didn't know Dottie then. I knew who she was. She was at my second Ironman and at the women's breakfast. I thought she was very self-assured. She spoke with authority.

It was Dottie who provided me with a greater sense of the gradual manner through which the two came to know each other. She wrote about it in an email some days after I left Celeste's Naples home:

Although Celeste and I met on "the Battlefield of Triathlon" it

---

1. Hawaiian Triathlon Corporation, "Bud Light Ironman Triathlon World Championship XI Race Results," October 14, 1989, http://www.ironman-hawaii.com/ergebnislisten/hawaii/im-hawaii1989.pdf.

became more than that. At first you sort of know she is there on "the Scene," but don't know her. You've heard her name but there is no real connection.

We rack our bikes at the beginning of a triathlon by age group and make our spot in the transition area "Our little Home away from Home." It includes organizing a lot of "Stuff" to cover the three legs of the triathlon: swim, bike and run.

My first memory of Celeste was at a race. She was very high strung. She was shouting at someone next to her designated number area that they were intruding on her space.

In many ways we came from "The Opposite Ends of a Bell Shaped Curve." I was quite intimidated that she had been on *Jeopardy*, had lived all over the world and had homes in three different locations.

We became much better known to each other through races and mutual friends, especially Judy.

Of course, Judy. In their memoirs, both Dottie and Celeste emphasize the importance of Judy Flannery to their journeys. While Dottie does not indicate when she first met Judy, Celeste does. Writing about "Wilkes-Barre" in 1988 Celeste recalls a casual exchange between two women:

Standing at bike check out at nationals, I heard one woman say to the woman next to me, "I finished 2:38." The woman next to me said that was great. I found out later that the woman next to me was Judy and she did 2:28.

Many studies suggest that memory does not consist of a complete record of the reality of the past, awaiting recollection by the future self. As life unfolds, the mind, swayed by the winds of personal and contextual whim, stores away select elements of real experience and forgets others. There was a reason why Celeste cut that exchange out and pasted it in her mental scrapbook for future recollection. She did not know that the woman next to her was Judy Flannery and that Judy would become a good friend. I wonder what about that moment kept the exchange fresh enough to recall sometime later.

It was a recognizable "Wilkes-Barre" tee-shirt that jogged Celeste's memory when Judy boarded her plane en route to Kona for the 1988 Ironman triathlon, Celeste's first. Judy's clothing also provided Celeste with a starting point for the first of many conversations. They drove the bike course together, and both attended the masters women's breakfast, which had consolidated into an annual tradition. For Judy and Celeste, the shared experiences of Hawaii in 1988 became the foundation for many more shared experiences. Having received the gift of aero bars from her family the following Christmas, Celeste needed some direction:

I spoke with Judy just after the holidays, who indicated that "soon we start getting ready for next season. We'll do this and that and then get ready for Ironman."

As Celeste recounts, her athletic endeavors multiplied and diversified in large part due to Judy's initiative. Together they competed in a range of events including duathlon, which consists of cycle and run legs.

So, I raced another season and another Ironman, an Ironman that did not seem so strange. The second Ironman, I finished maybe five minutes slower than the first.

The newness continued. Judy and I went to Crawfishman. We stayed with my brother. It had odd distances. And it was very cold. We each won different age groups and we did it again. That was probably the most extraordinary event.

I did not understand why Judy would do duathlon, but I started—I did a few and did OK. There was a saying in triathlon that the sport was a bike-run. But in order to get to your bike, you had to swim.

Yet it is the specific history of the sport of triathlon that gave shape to Celeste's multisport adventure. It also led to her first direct contact with Dottie. The International Triathlon Union (ITU)—founded in 1989 with hopes of Olympic recognition for the sport—furnished a whole set of enticing new goals for Judy, Celeste and Dottie. The season revolved around qualification for the national triathlon championships, where, from 1990, they strove to qualify for the ITU Triathlon World Championships:

The Golden Years of triathlon for me seem to have been 1987–2005, more or less. I was a constant at national championships, always garnering a place on Team USA.

Actually, that's not true. No, I did not make it on Team USA at first.

In '89 the first world championship was in Avignon and I didn't qualify. Nobody really cared. Nobody really knew about it until Australia in 1991. I had a bad race in Houston. I didn't do well, and I didn't care. Qualification was not within my reach. I had to be near the top of my age group.

I continued to go to Nationals. At the 1990 national championships in Gary, Indiana, I forgot my paper to qualify for the worlds at Orlando. They took the top eighteen for the worlds, figuring that with a larger field they could bargain with a city that would want the tourist money. But I did not make Worlds, that year at Disney World.

Judy did. Of course, I never expected to compete with Judy. Judy didn't care how I finished, just that I tried my best.

8. Masters in Motion

Elaborating in conversation on her involvement in the 1991 ITU Triathlon World Championships, Celeste shared an anecdote. It felt familiar, like an advertising jingle. Later I checked—it was almost word for word the same as a passage in her memoir. For me, this underlines the extent to which the story she tells about her life is selective. Why did she preserve this moment, and in this way? Why re-visit it over and over? Like the frozen memory of her first encounter with Judy, possibly the significance of the incident lies in the function it plays in the story that makes sense of her life:

The following year, the Worlds were in Australia, narrowing the field to those who could afford the time off and cost of the trip. I placed seventh at nationals and was set to go to the Ironman in Hawaii for my third race there. I remember the phone call:

"Celeste? This is Tim Yount from TriFed. You have just gotten a move down slot for Gold Coast, Australia. Do you accept?"

I leaned over to my to-do list for the next day and crossed out RIDE 100 MILES. "Of course," I said. The two events [*Ironman and the ITU Triathlon World Championships*] were a week apart. I would never have attempted both. Now, maybe. Then, no.

Celeste may have been aware of Dottie at Ironman qualifying races, and the Ironman breakfast in 1989, but her first clear memory of interacting with Dottie is linked directly to her first international triathlon. For Celeste, the choice to go to Australia was obvious, but for Dottie— who also qualified—it was less clear. As Celeste explains:

Dottie was talking to George. She didn't know whether to go. He asked what she liked the most about Ironman, to which she replied, "the women's breakfast." So George sponsored a masters women's breakfast at the [*ITU*] world championships and started a new tradition. He was the only man attending in the early years.

Dottie and I started talking on the phone a lot when preparing the women's breakfast. She can talk a lot on the phone. So we began to talk and became friends after that and saw each other frequently and became close friends.

As Celeste affirms, the masters women's breakfasts hosted by the Dorions at the ITU Triathlon World Championships proved as memorable as the Hawaiian ones:

The first world championship women's breakfast was the best breakfast. We sat in our age groups, had photos with our age groups. The food was wonderful. There was no entertainment, but we didn't need it. It was wonderful to be a part of such a good thing.

Somewhere in the mass of Dottie's papers I found an impressive leather embossed photo album. Arranged neatly within its pages are photos from the breakfasts. The photos feature groups of women wearing the uniforms of assorted national teams. The women are gathered around plaques that announce whether they are in the 45–49, 50–54, 55–59 age group and so on. While the composition of each photo is formal, the women appear relaxed. They grin and wave. Their eyes speak to someone off camera, and tilted heads react silently to jokes we will never hear.

In conversation, Dottie explained that she sent photos by mail to each breakfast attendee. Indeed, the Dorions paid attention to detail— each year printing event-specific napkins. "Who would have wiped the remnants of pastry and icing sugar off their fingers with those thoughtful mementos?" I wondered when I first came across them. As ITU world championships were held at diverse locations around the world, organizing such events took considerable effort. Writing in her memoir about the ITU breakfasts, Dottie recalls:

It was a challenge to find a restaurant nearby that could accommodate large gatherings, and to purchase local gifts in that country as

Judy Flannery (left) and Celeste holding the 50–54 age group plaque at the 1993 Masters Women's breakfast, held prior to the Manchester ITU Triathlon World Championships (Dottie Dorion Collection).

Dottie (front row, left) with 60–64 age group attendees at the 1994 Masters Women's Breakfast, held prior to the Wellington ITU Triathlon World Championships (Dottie Dorion Collection).

unique souvenirs for all the attendees. At Cancun in 1995 they received a special Mexican hand-woven wall hanging. On another occasion it was a metal triathlon ornament from Vermont.

For many women the breakfast was the highlight of their entire trip. Many women looked for ways to continue their friendships throughout the year and they decided to publish a newsletter. It started out called *No Name* newsletter and progressed by vote to *Masters in Motion*. All the women were invited to write articles and the response to "off season" was overwhelming. One woman living in a remote area told us she would rush to her mailbox for the delivery of the quarterly newsletter. It became a "down home" newsletter with heartfelt life stories, race experiences, recipes, training tips, testimonials, news about legislation, cartoons, Letters to the Editor, and a little tasteful gossip. The women were ever so grateful and many of the women still stay in contact to this day.

No Name. Most likely the lack of a name for the newsletter in the beginning was not intended to be meaningful. Yet those two words stand out to me as deeply relevant to the women who kept in touch through the newsletter. The breakfast was designed to foster and facilitate interaction between women whose efforts to become triathletes were compounded by the twin obstacles of gender and age. Contact with other masters women athletes appears to have promoted relief, encouragement and confidence. When Celeste tried to explain the personal significance of the breakfasts, she wrote about being seen as an independent person, about feeling visible. In many ways, the breakfasts, and the newsletter, made masters women triathletes visible as a group. In the beginning they had no name. As a result of the breakfasts and newsletter they came to define themselves as Masters in Motion.

It seems more than appropriate that Dottie and Celeste connected directly in the context of organizing the first ITU masters women's breakfast, an event that consolidated a new collective identity for women triathletes over forty.

Masters women triathletes did not gain collective visibility immediately and organically. Women aged over forty were almost like strays, who ventured into a world made for men, and in which younger women had begun to find a place. There was no guarantee, at the start of the 1990s, that the identities forged within the protective shell of the masters women's breakfasts at Kona would solidify into a recognizable new demographic across the triathlon world. The continuation of the breakfasts within the Olympic arm of the sport affirms the impact and the promise of the Hawaiian precursor, while the title given to the newsletter—Masters in Motion—seems to signal the maturation of the new collective identity.

George suffered a stroke prior to the 1995 ITU triathlon world championships breakfast at Cancun, Mexico, necessitating Dottie's nursing skills and attention. For the first time, the Dorions stepped back from their central role in the ITU breakfasts. Preparing to hand the breakfast over to other organizers in 1996, Dottie drafted a "Mistress of Ceremonies" guide, emphasizing the importance of the event for age group women rather than elite athletes. Despite her advice the breakfast began to reflect different interests and identities:

In 2013, many decades after the first Women's Breakfast, women gathered in London for a Women's Tea; it offered the same network and socializing opportunity, but in a different format. The male triathletes tried a breakfast one year and it was NOT successful.

While the focus of the breakfasts may have shifted, masters women athletes emerged as not just a visible community, but as a valuable demographic in the newly formalized sport. The camaraderie emerging from and repeatedly boosted through the breakfasts and newsletters

Posing for age group podium photographs, such as this one from the 1994 Tri-Fed National Amateur Championship, was a common experience for Dottie (left) (Dottie Dorion Collection).

fostered an annual routine of training and competition that took Dottie, Celeste, Judy and their peers across the continent and around the globe. Many masters women triathletes became core participants in a relatively niche sporting lifestyle on which the Olympic arm of the sport and new commercial enterprises relied for their existence.

Celeste evoked a sense of this lifestyle when she showed me some photographs.

Here is a picture of our age group at the first women's breakfast on the Gold Coast. Judy drove on the wrong side of the street the whole time. We had a lot of adventures.

Worlds that year was a premier event not to be repeated. Ever. Just as Nationals at Hilton Head was the perfect Nationals, never to be repeated. Ever (due to a hurricane). At the 1991 Worlds our race uniforms were a design of the American flag, so high at the hips—they were bathing suits then—that Judy remarked how much the nuns would have disapproved.

I remember it was a pretty crummy race for me. There were sharks—I never looked at how I did.

Dottie (left), George, and Tina Braam from Canada at the 1994 Masters Women's Breakfast (Dottie Dorion Collection).

Judy did intervals before the race. She said, "I'd like to get a podium spot." At the awards ceremony you were told that if you got an award, to leave the room before the previous group and a man marched in front of you as you walked on stage, and they raised the flag. It was like the Olympics.

It was fun with Judy. I needed to go home because it was our anniversary. My husband said stay. We bought hats—cowboy hats. Right next to us was a nude beach and women sat around with boobs out. My friend lost a watch and one of these women was helping to look and her boobs were swinging. We decided we would pull down our bathing suits in the car, for fun. People were going to take pictures but collapsed with laughter. We did a side trip to the Blue Mountains. Judy always laid this out. She always had everything planned.

Soon the Worlds became the peak of every year's training. We'd go about a week before the event. In 1993 we were in Manchester, UK, in 1995 at Cancun. Judy and I would room together. The head of the tour company liked Judy, and so we always got the best rooms.

So we'd settle into our hotel room. We would put our bikes together. We would unpack and try to make order of a simple room with two beds;

Dottie managed a smile at the 1994 Wellington ITU Triathlon World Championships despite the cold and windy conditions (courtesy Arthur Klap).

with two large hard shell bike cases, uniforms, triathlon gear, and, as Judy called them, civilian clothes. The bathrooms need not be described.

We'd greet old friends and make new ones. There was a massage staff member and a chiropractor and a doctor, and I spent a lot of time with the middle fellow there. There was always a specific hotel for Team

USA. The whole team would stay together in the same hotel. Old home week sums it up.

We would drive the course. We would study the course. We would plan our logistics. Then on Thursday night there was always a Parade of Nations. We had parade shirts and shorts and jackets and caps. The American flag was always taken by a photo happy group of older women. We would line up behind a child dressed in the national garb of the country in question, carrying a large fancy sign with the name of the country—as is done in the Olympics. And we would walk the mile or two of the routes that wound through the busiest streets in town and we would make noise, generally being obnoxious but interpreted by onlookers as patriotic fervor. Except after 9/11. We did "respectful" then, many of us aware of the targets on our backs.

While on vacation after the 1994 ITU Triathlon World Championships at Wellington, Dottie and George enjoyed a fishing trip with some other athletes; one of Dottie's favorite memories of their time in New Zealand (Dottie Dorion Collection).

There was a pasta party after the Parade, but we never went. Judy's groupies did not like to stand in line for food. On Fridays we had a team meeting. On Saturdays we got our gear together and turned in our bikes to the transition. Oh, I forgot that toward the beginning of the week we had a time slot in which to register as a country and to pick up our packets, as well as any—and there always was—thing to buy with the word TRIATHLON and the name of the country who was our host.

What was not to love?

8. Masters in Motion

Race day was the least of it. I usually cooked oatmeal in the bath-room and drank my coffee while I read, sitting on a towel on the cold hard floor. Judy slept in, drinking only coffee. Paula, my later roommate, always had a Diet Pepsi. Judy and Paula always won their age groups at Worlds. I did not podium till my '60s. Whose advice would *you* follow?

Judy didn't have sugar. She was very particular about what she ate. She wouldn't eat something because she felt that it was too salty. Pasta was the thing that we always ate at that time. I never had a weight prob-lem at all. Before my second Ironman I read an article that said you're overweight if you stand in front of the mirror and jump up and down and everything jiggles. I went to the doctor and went on the South Beach diet. I went without carbohydrates and sugar for two weeks. It was awful. Then I realized I was fifty-two and my metabolism had slowed down and I couldn't eat as much as I did. We weren't doing abs and weights. We weren't conscious about our bodies.

I liked wearing the casual clothes. My husband once asked, "Do you have any clothes without something written on it?" In Hawaii there was a company called Zoot. They had spectacular clothes. I bought the clothes because they were cool. They were neon. Neon was big in the '80s. We always got free kit [*"kit" is triathlon vernacular for clothing and sometimes essential accessories*], in those days but we didn't go out in those things. You wore them for running or biking, or for walking around at Kona. Anything I bought at Ironman I wore. I probably wore them in Denver. I have finisher's tee shirts I never wore or wore only once. I saw a cleaning lady wearing one of them and she said it was in a packet that I gave away. I still have my Ironman shirts, but the graphics are definitely dated.

Judy put a little photo album together for me. There were a lot of photos: a Bud Light race; Chicago, a qualifying race for nationals; the age group winners in 1992. This was what triathlon was like. I spent a lot of time in motels. We were sneaking out of the hotel to train. That was how it was.

I used to go to a bike shop or have them put the bike together for me. Sometimes I would have someone from the hotel help, then I learned how to do it eventually. I had a bike shop show me some things and just learned how by doing it. Judy was so pleased. She said, "I'm so proud of you putting your bike together."

At the Manchester Worlds we stayed with a lady who was so excited and took us to meet the mayor. We were in our uniform, and we had a photo outside the mayor's place while he posed with a bike.

Celeste with her bike in the transition area at the 1995 Cancun ITU Triathlon World Championships (Dottie Dorion Collection).

That was the year Judy realized what a big deal she was, 1993. She became concerned about winning. Two French women beat her, but she was stopped by a volunteer, because the number on her bike was flapping, so she had a stop-and-start penalty. It was not fair. She got third place and wasn't happy about that.

Another time we went to Ferrara, Italy, and to a bicycle camp in the Dolomites. After the race, we went on a tour to Rome and Florence and we were in a hotel room and Judy said, "It's always you and me." She was my roommate for almost ten years from 1988 to 1997.

Both Celeste and Dottie began to tire of the circuit. Celeste paused after flicking through the photo album Judy gave her:

As we got older, we got disenchanted with the post race hoopla. In our forties and fifties though? We were there to do it all. A big deal was to trade part of your uniform with a competitor of another country. The only time I ever did that was at Guernica. I could not resist the natty Italian asking me to trade parade shirts. Unabashed, I took mine off and he gave me his. I smelled like B.O. for the rest of the night.

Nope. Going to Worlds and swimming and biking and running with the top triathletes on the planet through some of the world's most

Although they lived in different states, Celeste and Judy traveled together to events cross the United States and around the world. Here Judy (left) and Celeste fit in some swim training before the 1993 Manchester ITU Triathlon World Championship (Celeste Callahan Collection).

glamorous real estate fills my memory boxes with experiences few people can begin to share.

Dottie also lost interest in the circuit and its associated lifestyle as well:

In my mid-sixties National races and World ones began to lose their luster. The usual suspects were always there which, at first, had been high school reunion-like fun. Later it seemed like stagnation. The hoopla, as well as getting to the race meetings and turning in our bikes and registration and middle of the night oatmeal began to pale in their once-upon-a-time glory.

In short, the circuit was getting old. I began to like the local races with which I had never bothered and from which I could be in my own tub by noon with a bike that did not have to be shipped by sea, at what seemed like the cost of a college semester.

I had come full circle.

The appeal of the global circuit did not last, but reading and hearing the stories Dottie and Celeste tell about this phase in their journey, it seems that the clues they have scattered throughout their memoirs are leading me ever nearer to whatever their (as yet undeclared) purpose happens to be. The journey we are on is not purely personal in nature. The memoirs are not simply about their respective transformations into athletes. It has something to do with the Masters in Motion women.

That Dottie is interested in the obstacles and opportunities that confront those women when they set themselves athletic goals, is evident from the importance she attributes to the breakfasts. But there are other signs that Dottie is concerned about the barriers to female participation in sport. The earliest memory Celeste has of Dottie, relates to the way in which the latter secured a slot at the 1989 Ironman triathlon. It is instructive that like her first encounter with Judy, Celeste also freeze-framed this moment for subsequent recollection. She urged me to ask Dottie about it, who complied:

I went to the Crawfishman Triathlon. I met several people also doing the race. I had a friend from Texas who had driven there all by herself. She got there and found they didn't have the age group divisions she planned on. She thought there were five year age increments, and found out it was ten years. That was often the case for older women. I felt badly because she had sacrificed a lot. I had it in my mind to tell her to stay close and I would look out for her. But I did win it.

When they came to giving the Ironman slot awarded to me, I said,

"I'm not going to accept. I'm going to give it to Joanne because she thought the conditions were different."

Everyone gasped—I gave away an Ironman slot! I didn't think anything more because I thought she deserved it. Then two days later a package came in the mail from Ironman and it was a lottery slot for me. So we both got it.

Embedded in this account, is evidence of Dottie's predilection to look for solutions when she identifies specific needs, in this case highlighting the limiting and obscuring assumptions that faced mature sporting women in the 1980s. Dottie resolved the situation by doing what she could, surrendering her place and in the process highlighting the inequality. Celeste thought the gesture was "remarkable." She was also impressed by Dottie's leadership in establishing the 1991 ITU women's breakfast tradition at the Gold Coast world championships. At that point, Dottie's initiative was both admirable and foreign to Celeste.

While Dottie and Celeste do not directly articulate the origins and catalysts for their friendship, their memoirs imply that they became firmer friends as the social bonds between the Masters in Motion women deepened. Dottie and Celeste became more aware of each other just as the breakfast women began to see themselves as a collective entity. The 1993 ITU Triathlon World Championships took place in Manchester, England, the same year that Celeste moved to London. Dottie competed at Manchester and returned to England the following year after Celeste was diagnosed with cancer. Dottie and Celeste together caught up with mutual triathlon friends during that visit. The following year, the cancer scare became the catalyst for a new social tradition on American soil, as Celeste explains:

The significant part about having cancer is that everyone laughs at your jokes and treats you like a queen. Everyone loves you. Right after I had cancer, we had Camp Vail. Everyone came in 1995. Camped all over the house. "Exact Queen" became my nickname at the time. We had a race outside, running through the snow to a tree and back. I think Dottie fell. She was a good sport. At Camp Vail we went to this wheat grass thing. In the morning we would go and have wheat grass. I read about it when I had cancer. It was awful.

Dottie says more about "Camp Vail," in a discussion of winter ski trips by some of the women triathletes to Vail, Colorado. In her account, the gatherings appear as the focus of heart-warming memories for all those who attended.

In the winter, we triathlete ladies camped out at Celeste's home in

Vail, Colorado, on what became known as, "Camp Vail Out of Control." We had that on our tee shirts. We were never quite sure if there would be ten of us, or thirty of us. Some came for a few days and slept wherever there was a bed or sleeping bags on the floor, and others were just for the day. It made no difference. The activities for the core group consisted of having some kind of green algae drink at a local store to start the day. Other activities consisted of all levels of skiing and various groups took off for the day: downhill, X-country, snowshoeing, heliport skiing, etc. We skied all day at various levels of competence, prepared meals (by designated teams), and slept in beds or on the floor at night. Judy, a "Team Leader" always had healthy meals and her cookies could be a meal in themselves. However, no matter the meal, Judy always had a glass of red wine. That allowed us to follow our "Champion" and always have a glass or two of red wine.

Celeste was dubbed the "Queen of Vail". Participants in the mid–1990 gatherings regularly created personalized items of clothing and accessories for the queen to wear (Dottie Dorion Collection).

Post dinner, we always had story time. This included fun reminiscences, tales of misadventures at triathlons and several members telling jokes. Judy had an incredible knack for telling jokes and most of them were a little "off color." This always surprised us knowing her strict Catholic background. Also, we had a contest when coming to Camp Vail. We gave a prize for the person who brought the least clothes in the smallest carry bag. Judy won every time and yet she always had appropriate clothes and did no laundry on site.

One true story Judy repeated many times, to our delight, went like this: Early on Sunday mornings Judy rode long distances with a group of men. This was a regular ride that went on for many years. The men on

Some of the 1995 Camp Vail participants joined Celeste (left) when she sampled wheatgrass juice, which was reported to be good for cancer survivors. Their verdict on the taste appears to be in the negative (Celeste Callahan Collection).

the ride kept asking Judy if she had a husband, wondering, "What husband would allow his wife out every weekend to ride a hundred miles or more with a group of guys?" Finally, one day Judy had heard enough of this and decided to take the whole group of riders up to her bedroom to prove, once and for all, she really did have a husband. Her husband was sound asleep in their bed when he awoke to a group of strangers standing around the bed and Judy saying, "See, there he is, I told you so."

Clearly Camp Vail was memorable and fun for all involved. Clearly, also, Judy represented a central feature of Camp Vail activities. Fun stories aside, Camp Vail was also a point of connection for women who achieved personal transformation through sport, and who hoped to assist in the sporting journeys of other women. Writing about Judy's role in strengthening her links with Celeste, Dottie indicates that she was not alone in her wish to address the obstacles to equal participation by women, especially masters and senior women, in the sport:

Judy had been the equalizer for both of us. We became much better known to each other through races and mutual friends, especially Judy.

In 1995, all the participants had "Camp Vail Out of Control" tops to wear (Dottie Dorion Collection).

We also started to develop mutual interests in Tri-Fed, and the lack of women's equality and opportunities.

Dottie and Celeste voluntarily and separately tell their version of one particular story regarding Judy, who took on the role of first chair of the USA Triathlon (formerly known as Tri-Fed) Women's Commission in 1995. Dottie's memoir provides some context:

All of us were involved in The Women's Commission of U.S.A. Triathlon and Judy was the Chairwoman. We decided we really needed a symbol representing "Our" organization, which could be utilized on letterheads and tee shirts. We faxed back and forth and decided on the outline of a woman runner. The figure became a little problematic because "she" didn't look like a female. I communicated to Judy that the figure needed either long hair or boobs. Judy sent her back with boobs and so she remains to this day.

During a conversation at Naples, Celeste pointed to two women and a piece of paper in one of her photographs, explaining:

That's Judy and that's me, and that's from the Women's Commission. Judy made the logo. She put boobs on it. She thought it was funny. They still use this logo.

132

8. Masters in Motion

The logo acts as a reminder of an era when women, particularly masters women, represented a relatively small proportion of the triathlon population. Though many enjoyed materially comfortable lives, triathlon offered these women new opportunities to explore their athletic potential and to savor the rewards of setting and achieving personal goals, and through the regular cycle of multisport goals to develop independent lifestyles, social groups and identities. Considering the focus of the tales that Dottie and Celeste tell about this period, it almost seems that the final stages of the personal metamorphoses they describe occurred as a result of the simultaneous coalescence of isolated pre–Title IX women triathletes into a community. To me, the deliberately feminized running figure in the Women's Committee logo appears to symbolize this new community; I imagine the figure with Judy at its heart and Dottie at its head. It also resonates with the merriment that characterized their interactions, as well as their strengthening belief that triathlon should and could offer a pathway not only to their own personal development, but also to the collective progress of their kind. It is clear to me by now that the memoir project has a great deal to do with this vision.

9

Redemption

Judy Flannery stars in the memories Dottie and Celeste share of the Masters in Motion women and the active lifestyle they enjoyed. But Judy was more than just another face in the photographs that freeze-frame fleeting moments from those days.

At the very least, Judy inspired simply because she seemed so capable; she was widely recognized as a competitive athlete. In early 1997 both Celeste and Judy trained for a Powerman race at Birmingham. Powerman was a non–ITU duathlon brand with a range of events around the world. For Judy, "Powerman" represented part of her preparation for the Ride Across America, which she decided to do after hearing about Celeste's "ghastly" attempt at the epic event. All who knew Judy expected that she would win her age group at the Birmingham Powerman, as Celeste's account suggests:

Powerman was on the Easter weekend. It was a very difficult duathlon. It was held in Birmingham and had a horrible hill. I flew there, and Judy was there, and Rita was there. Rita Sharpe laughed a lot. She was good fun. There was Harry. He was older than all of us. He was married to a woman who died of lung cancer, when he fell apart. He just followed Judy around; a darling guy but he needed help. Judy would get his tickets otherwise he wouldn't go. He was very funny. We all stayed together, and we did this race.

I started with Judy and ran with her for the first mile. I was so excited, I said to her, "I stayed with you for the first mile!"

At the end of the race everyone was saying, "Judy got beat," "Judy got beat." She was fine about it and said, "Well she ran six minute miles!" The announcer gave Judy a bigger to-do than the other woman at the Awards Ceremony. She said it sounded like her epitaph.

But Judy offered more than just an athletic role model. Directly and indirectly Judy encouraged Masters in Motion women to think more broadly about the sporting landscape in which they found fun, challenge, meaning and direction. She was central to another shift in Celeste's goal setting, but the new goal Judy inspired was not an athletic one. Celeste was not restless after another move. The step was not about another personal metamorphosis through athletic endeavor, but it did lead to her further evolution beyond the role of daughter, wife and mother. The new goal became a mission, as Celeste recounts:

I was fifty four years old that cold morning, April 1, 1997. I was driving to the bike shop and wanted to tell Judy that I was following her instructions. She, my best friend from triathlon and my roomie for all the worlds and national events, was the first President of the Women's Commission at USA Triathlon. In February she asked me to be the Rocky Mountain Representative. I don't like busy work but on the same day as the Powerman Awards ceremony—Easter Sunday—we went to Mass and we sat in the parking lot and she told me about all she had to do in April.

"What do I have to do?" I asked.

"Just get women into triathlon."

So I talked the *Denver Post* into a dab on a sidebar: Anyone interested in trying her first triathlon, call this number. I wanted to tell Judy all about it. I wanted her to give me a gold star.

I expected her answering machine when I called her the Tuesday after Easter. Thinking about it, I bet I am the only one in the world, except for maybe her husband, who knew that Judy was not at S.O.M.E that day.

"Why aren't you at S.O.M.E.?"

A laugh. "I'm waiting for the electrician."

The next evening, both Tom Brokaw and Dan Rather would end the news with reports about Judy's death, saying that the day before she was killed on her bike, she was working at a soup kitchen called So Others May Eat [*S.O.M.E.*], in Washington, D.C.

So April 2, 1997, was the day that began, I guess you could say, the immortality of Judy Flannery—a fifty-seven-year-old mother of five grown children, a wife of a Washington lawyer, the companion of two Irish setters whose names do not, at the moment, register. Connor and Roan, maybe.

Judy wanted women in triathlon. She did not care how you placed. She just wanted you to "go like hell" and be happy in the process. The stories of waiting for Judy at the end of a race are legend. She would find every woman she could, to ask how their day went. Maybe, I see now, there was a purpose for all this *bon homie*. Or *bon woman*. Until now—or rather, then—I just figured she was being friendly. Maybe she knew she was soon, uh, checking out and wanted to leave a bit of herself behind with all the women whose paths crossed hers. Or she wanted to make sure that she crossed theirs.

So as soon as she knew that I was starting a group of women to teach them triathlon, that this group would begin with sixty and climax to five hundred before exploding into several different training clubs, she did. Check out.

While Celeste narrates Judy's death in the context of an unfolding new direction in her triathlon endeavors, a new direction tied intrinsically to Judy's mission to involve more women in the sport, Dottie learned of Judy's accident out of the blue. In her memoir she articulates feelings of shock, grief and loss:

Judy. Judy was always there. We competed in what seemed like hundreds of triathlons around the world. Judy Flannery always finished First and we (the rest of us) survived to finish as best we could. No matter where we were in the pack, Judy was always there, waiting for us at the Finish Line. She cheered on the fastest of us and the slowest of us, and often her inspiration kept us going to the finish. No matter what, Judy was there.

Judy was a modest person. She received many coveted awards, trophies, and honors and yet never mentioned them or felt superior to others. She encouraged so many fledgling beginners in a diversity of sports and transported those who needed help to get to races; Judy was "Mother Hen" to all of us. In other words, whenever someone needed a helping hand she was there.

Judy was always there until she wasn't.

It is difficult to this day to deal with this loss and being a Hospice nurse [*Dottie says more about hospice nursing later*], one might think I have all the answers. I don't.

There are phone calls you wish you never had to take. It was about Judy. Judy was out biking with two friends when she was hit and killed instantly by a car. Judy had been riding in the middle and the other two riders were unharmed. The silence on my end of the phone lasted what seemed like minutes because the shock is so great you can't speak.

Many days of grief followed and then her funeral, which had hundreds of mourners and a trail of bicycles following the funeral procession. All of us cried until we couldn't cry any more. Now we are decades later, and we still mourn her. To me, a sudden death is much more difficult to resolve the grief, as I also found in the death of children. There

9. Redemption

Judy Flannery on a hike in Tasmania following the 1994 ITU Duathlon World Championships (Dottie Dorion Collection).

is one saying that Judy had repeated at various times over many years, "When your time comes, your time comes." Her time came much too soon, and I try and remember she is at peace, and the best we can do is carry on her work with women in sport and remember...

Dottie concludes her memoir chapter about Judy:

Judy is not here, but she is truly with us in spirit.

Judy's unforeseen passing added personal significance to the tentative steps Celeste had taken at Judy's behest, to encourage more women to take up triathlon. In her memoir Celeste explains that, although hesitant about becoming involved in "busy work," she followed through on her promise to Judy. A surprising number of women responded to the small announcement Celeste placed in the Denver Post *so she and two coaches, Rose Weber and Kerstin Weuhle, went ahead with the advertised "start up" meeting. Their aim was to prepare the women who turned up for their debut triathlon, which would be the women only Danskin Triathlon, scheduled for August:*

We felt grief for a friend—a lot of it was shock. This is probably why Jesus had such success, because people with shock begin new movements. We began new movements because of Judy.

Beyond Triathlon

The first meeting was four hours after Judy died.

It was an effort to concentrate on the women in my living room that night. I thought of telling them about the accident but decided it would not be a big favor to the distaff side of the sport. At the end of the meeting, one of the two women who led the class with me passed around a sign up sheet with the initials CWW on top: Callahan, me; Weber for Rose; Weuhle for Kerstin. Team CWW we became, later known with the moniker Colorado Wild Women that seventeen years later was trademarked officially.

I planned for one season only. CWW. The three of us, joined by Susie who brought with her Colorado Team Survivor, took the women riding. Kerstin's husband checked all tires. My favorite newbie memory is that of a rear bike fender with an Evian bottle bungee-corded on top. We brought the women to the beach and told them to get in and feel the water. We walked them through the paces, especially about what to do the day before and the morning of the event. With four months to go, we had no time to teach from scratch. I had said in my ad that, if they could swim from one end of the pool to the other at gunpoint, ride around the block without falling off, and run as though from fire, they could do a triathlon. My deal was to tell them that, if they wanted to finish, they could: upright and with a pulse.

I got a guy, my coach Dave, to help. I told him, "You can't talk too low. You can't assume anything. Tell them how to put on a wetsuit." He was very good and showed them.

Two weeks before the Denver Danskin race, I got the park to let us do a practice swim at the beach. In those days before cancer got to be big business, it was a guilt qualm with the men.

I saw a ranger: "Can a group of breast cancer survivors (although we were just one third such) have a practice?"

"Of course," he answered.

Later, as both we, and breast cancer, got bigger, our practices cost us up to $2,000. We needed permits and signs and ambulances and rangers. In the summer of 1997: zip.

Every one of us started the race that first year. Everyone finished. The next week we had a pot luck at my house. "Can we do this next year?" someone asked. But "Can we call it a 'team'? We have never before been on a team."

So someone designed a logo. We arranged for an embroidery shop to do a mock-up for us for $150, costing just $5 a bathing suit to make up a uniform.

9. Redemption

The year following Judy's death, her daughter Erin came out to Denver with an LA film crew to film us at the next Danskin. *Judy's Time* went on to be an award-winning documentary about Judy and her life and death as told through the eyes of her children, who had no idea what she was up to when she was off on her bike.

We dedicated CWW to Judy. Our color was hot pink, which many mistook for cancer. "No," I told them one Kick Off. "One time Judy and I were at the baggage carousel at O'Hare: 'Is that yours?' I asked hopefully. 'Now, Celeste,' I quoted Judy as saying, 'Do I ever go *anywhere* without a pink plastic ribbon tied to my bags?'"

I told Kick Off that I mentioned the incident to everyone the night before the funeral. Erin got the plastic pink ribbon from Judy's bike bag, and we tied it to the handles of her coffin, so that "wherever she was going, she could find her way there."

On the third anniversary of Judy's death, I woke up to go get the newspaper out in front. On the high wrought iron gate were one hundred pink plastic ribbons that had been mailed to each member in a newsletter. In the middle of the night, each had stealthily tied one to the gate.

Later we would give out the pink ribbons at bike clinics to show which riders belonged to us so that we would not boss around ancillary people. And at practices, we used the pink ribbon as a finish line.

Judy never really left.

Memories of Judy continue to weave through Celeste's accounts of CWW activities, but the women-only training group developed a life of its own:

We were the only game in town. We got more coaches. We had swim coaches and bike coaches and run coaches. We got more equipment. We charged only as much as it cost to train. Our numbers grew like Topsy, not because of the sport, but through word of mouth, because they heard what the sport DID for them. They called because a husband had just left. Or they were turning fifty or sixty. Or they had to lose a hundred pounds. Or they had diabetes and the doctor said to exercise. Or they felt lonely. Or they did not know who they were.

My goal was to teach women self-reliance. Our target was the woman who said, "NO WAY! I could never do THAT!" having her do "that" became the hill we would die on. I would die on.

The newbies were our reason for being, I told them, I told everyone. So I kept them after the general meeting each January and told them about me, about how I was not allowed to do sports, about my Epiphany while folding diapers, my first masters swim, the girls' bike with the basket—or was it a baby seat?—all of it. They nodded. They understood. Most were over whatever age it had to be to be graduated from high school or college before 1978. Most did not play sport before attending this Kick Off. They felt that, if I could do it and maintain some sort of levity, so could they. And they did.

So we gave them a challenge: and for many years, that challenge was the Danskin Triathlon for the Susan B Komen Foundation. The first Sunday in August gave the women precisely seven months to learn how to leave the rec center bathroom and step onto the pool deck in a bathing suit, how to put their faces in the water, how to learn to swim in the pool, and then how to do the same in what we called the gravel pond. But they did it. Seven months was not a long time to train the legs to ride a bike and then walk to the car afterwards, not to mention the run. And the run? They drove across town in the 5:00 p.m. traffic and came to all the track workouts, the runs around Washington Park.

Dottie was the one who said don't do the race with them. So on the first Sunday in August, I would get up at 4:00 in the morning, be the first one to a race site that would hold 2,000 athletes and half as many volunteers, and set up our tent and wait for the problems to arrive. And arrive they would. "I left my timing chip at home!" "I just started my period." "My bike got a flat just between here and the car."

I would tell them that they needed to be there when transition opened. If a race started at 7:30, they needed to be parking their cars no later than 5:30. I told them, "You will find that when you get in the line to check in, it will already be a mile long."

Soon the other coaches would appear with their emotional and practical band aids. We got permission to walk around inside transition area as the sun was coming up and check on how things were laid out and listen to more drama. "Someone moved my bike and put hers in my place." A lot of women had breakdowns. We'd help them put their bikes together, and show them what they needed to do: "There are 3,000 bikes, how are you going to find the bike?" We got them to run from the water to the bike, from the bike rack to the bike exit.

Jacob Reservoir is fairly centrally located in the south east part of town. They had to swim half a mile to the right of the pier, bike inside the Reservoir grounds, and then run over the dam, which was fairly windy.

So we'd go out on the pier. And then it would be time for the fifteen waves of countdowns and encouragements and "get your faces in the water, now!" "Get used to the cold."

9. Redemption

The focus activity for CWW was the Danskin Denver Women's Triathlon held in early August every year. Team CWW members at the Denver Danskin race in 2000 are recognizable with their pink swim caps (Celeste Callahan Collection).

After all the swim waves were done, we would return to our tent and see that half our team had already finished. We'd drink and eat what we each had brought and stored in the tent. We would line up for a group picture. We would tell stories. We would cry.

We've had a lot of women who've overcome major difficulties and gone through personal journeys. We had a girl who was blind, who was a good runner and started doing triathlon with a guide. We had one woman join with two girls. One was a beautiful girl. One was over-weight. The woman joined with two girls to help the second one lose weight. The overweight girl did the triathlon and six weeks later she had a baby in the bathroom. That was a surprise!

One woman had glaucoma and she said, "You're the only ones who treat me like I'm alive."

There are so many stories about women worrying about their husbands and children. We had a girl saying, "What do we do with our children?" We had mini-triathlons to practice and one girl came with her man in a triathlon shirt and a stopwatch. We don't want them being told what to do. The women did not need to know whether or not they had fast twitch muscle fibers or how long an interval should be. They needed to know that someone *was listening to them* and that they *mattered*. We wanted women to stop and help each other.

I know all those things. I tell them, "It's empowering. You always put on your oxygen mask before you help someone else. I learned that when I went out and ran for twelve minutes. If I have time to go to the pool, then I can come back and do whatever my husband or children want. My husband didn't want me to do my first triathlon—the one for fun. He said, 'You'll be too tired to fix dinner.' I intentionally went to the grocery store and fixed dinner after." Other times I say, "I often seem to have a problem with my husband: 'The TV is too loud,' or 'I want to eat now.' But when I get to the eighteenth mile of the marathon, I always hit the wall, actually at the seventeenth mile. When I get to the eighteenth mile it all gets better." I tell them this is a way of getting past a problem. A woman who is older than me called before one race because her husband disappeared and she didn't know where he was, but he just went to get a movie camera to take pictures of her.

Those are just some of the stories. Of the 2,000 women, or more, who have crossed their first triathlon finish lines through us, we only had two not complete a race. In seventeen years! One had a health issue that would not let her swim. The other is from India. And she is still at it. She had not learned to ride a bike when she, at age forty-five, came to us. And she still cannot swim worth noting. But she tries. So we learned to tell them that, for some, the finish line would come later. It was keeping going that was key.

For all the attention Celeste vested in the many individual journeys of Team CWW members, the initiative itself contributed to Celeste's ongoing journey. CWW represents the start of a third metamorphosis in her personal journey as well as a notable landmark in her memoir's metaphorical trek into the unknown:

I would go home totally drained. I would want to talk, though. I would want to tell Dick all about it.

But the first Sunday in August was always the date of the International Golf Tournament at Castle Pines, and he was never home when I arrived by noon. That was OK. He had his thing, and I had mine. It is remarkable that I felt that we could be two individuals, each pursuing what interested us. Sport did that for me. Where once I would have whined, I now just took a nap. I once told someone that Dick was not my half, but he allowed me to be whole. And I meant it.

Celeste's use of the term "whole" is telling. Embedded in her oral and written narratives about CWW is the sentiment that having become self-enabled through her lonely struggles to master triathlon, Celeste could now enable others. She is both enabled and enabling. It is clear that the step from enabled woman athlete to enabler of other women is deeply significant:

The best part of my life, the part that has brought the greatest satisfaction has been Team CWW. The rewards were tsunami-ed toward me. The hugs, the tears, the confidences, the notes of thanks, and the presents at the Victory Party at the end of each year ... they all defined me, validated me. I would stand up in front of a room and *everyone would listen to me.* I was a hero. It was the time of my life. I got all the fame, which I have always thought was a pretty good gig. In 2004 I was awarded the USA Triathlon Volunteer of the Year Award. I felt—fulfilled.

The rewards continued to roll in, as Celeste recounts later in her memoir:

It is February of my seventy-first year, and we just had the seventeenth seasonal opening of Team CWW. We had been floundering, with splits and others wanting to coach and peeps wanting to form their own play groups; businesses.

This was my last-ditch effort, I had been thinking. We have a skinny show up at Kick Off, we muddle through the year, we send $100 to the seven or so businesses that sprang from us, and we announce we have accomplished our mission.

But at the Kick Off—standing room only.

After I returned home, I received a note from a single mom who could not do anything, the only one of our crowd who could not swim, bike or run:

> Hi Celeste, I just wanted to tell you what a pleasure it was meeting you today. I have never met a woman so inspiring—just glowing so beautifully—lined up perfectly with her truth. You made me feel like I was in exactly the right place with the right people.

And then, after a reunion for CWW grads from the early years, this:

> I was 55 when Sara Livingston talked me into joining CWW. It was a wonderful experience, but not just for me. There was a ripple effect after completing the Danskin Triathlon in 1999. My husband, daughter, and son were all there as spectators. My son told me in an awed voice that he was now going to call me "Studess"! As a result, my husband took swim lessons, our daughter joined CWW, and my son began mountain biking. A couple of friends joined CWW after hearing my tales about Dave's incredible swim coaching skills. After fifteen years my family is still reaping the benefits of a healthier lifestyle attributable to CWW. Thank you, Celeste.

The members used to give me a present at each Victory Party at the end of the season. One year I got a pewter box with CWW etched on the top. Inside were a hundred or so slips of paper on which each had written a message.

In her memoir Celeste reproduces many of the Team CWW messages written on those slips of paper. Aside from their flattering nature, I suspect that she selected notes that appealed to her because they highlight the same themes that are repeated throughout the memoir itself. Some are about balancing family life with training, a key struggle for Celeste herself:

You helped me focus on my training while focusing on my family.

Other testimonies relate to Celeste's perceived acceptance of the fears and concerns of CWW "newbies":

You took my mania about the open water seriously. You were there for me.

You never look down on anyone because you were once there yourself.

Having confronted a host of physical, personal and cultural obstacles in her journey from pre–Title IX mother and wife to triathlete Celeste brought credibility to her role as mentor:

I will always remember "If I can do it, you can do it!"

I always remember how you said, "If you can do this triathlon, you can do anything!"

Your leading by example pushed me to places I had never been. You changed my life. What can I NOT do now?

And for some CWW members both physical transformation and personal metamorphosis resulted from their experience of triathlon, just as it did for Celeste:

I always remember your smiling all the time, like you had this big secret you could not wait to share. Now that I have done a triathlon, I know what that secret is.

Thanks to you, I have the empowerment of completing a triathlon. Only the birth of my children and walking on the stage for my chiropractic degree are comparable.

Because of you, I have re-defined myself.

You changed my life.

Quite a few testimonies highlight Celeste's ability to draw on and make light of her triathlon experiences:

The tips you gave us at practice such as where to pee during triathlon.

9. Redemption

I will always remember your stories. They were funny, interesting—gross but funny (going on a towel).

Never in my wildest dreams did I think a woman of your stature would be telling me how to pee on a towel.

The testimonies are clearly meaningful for Celeste, seemingly offering proof that her journey, her challenges, and choices were relevant to other women as well. For a child of Catholic parents, and product of Catholic education, Celeste's final reflections on CWW in her memoir offers poignant evidence that her work with CWW proved affirming:

I never understood redemption until CWW. When one of them crosses the finish line after a very hard journey, I feel redeemed for everything I was told.

Over time, CWW developed appropriately a life of its own. It provided to other women things that were missing when Celeste began her metamorphosis; knowledge, support, and understanding of the specific and potentially prohibitive challenges that women—particularly masters women—face when they decide to attempt a triathlon. CWW helped to create a new reality, but in that new reality fewer members appreciated the extent to which the sporting landscape had changed since women like Celeste—and Judy and Dottie—had cleared the pathways along which they traveled.

Occasionally—through passing and incomplete comments in conversation—Celeste hinted that some members neither understood nor appreciated why she might view herself as a kind of "patron saint" to the training group. Misunderstanding also impacted on her relationship with one or two of the coaches who contributed to the training of CWW members over time:

There was one coach who distinguished herself with unprofessional tactics that had me fire her. Hell breaking loose is an understatement. But I learned a lot about life and keeping the high road and "what you are, speaks so loud I cannot hear what you say." So I got by. Flying colors.

CWW was not Celeste's only attempt to honor Judy's wish to encourage more women to embrace the sport of triathlon. In fact, CWW represented a spontaneous response to a broader initiative championed by Judy and Dottie—the USA Triathlon Women's Commission. First proposed in 1993, the idea of establishing a Women's Commission under the aegis of the national governing body for the sport, USA Triathlon (USAT), only became a reality in 1995. In the same year that Judy died, Celeste became involved in the Women's Commission, and contributed a section to its first instruction manual, based on her experience with

CWW. She also raised money to aid the work of the Women's Commission under the appropriately named Judy Flannery Memorial Fund and set up an Award aimed at recognizing women who embodied the values and leadership demonstrated by Judy. Celeste's participation in the Women's Commission represented another aspect of her transformation from enabled to enabler.

I was a Rocky Mountain regional representative on the Women's Commission, and I didn't know what I was supposed to do. We started with raising money. At the Women's Breakfast the following year, we presented the first Spirit of Judy Flannery Award. We got a statue. And Dottie said I could choose who should receive the Award. I chose Dottie. I had George there, and she was surprised.

It was meant to be for a woman who had a good athletic career and also gave back to the sport. That was certainly Dottie.

Celeste's work on the Women's Commission, and, in particular, her work with CWW aligned well with USAT objectives. In 2005 Celeste encountered the opportunity to deepen her role in triathlon governance and further expand her contribution to the sport:

I guess I was well known and a friend, Valerie, was president of the board of USAT at one stage. The [*USAT*] representative of the regions I would, uh, represent resigned. They needed someone to fill prior to the next election. They were all men. They needed a woman. A few other women were there as regional representatives. I have an impressive CV although people think more of me than I deserve. I suppose compared to some of these people I have. So I got a call.

My children probably do not deserve the grief I give them for categorizing me as non-focusing. I have trouble with hard ideas, such as business financials. So I do not listen. So, yes, I mostly do not focus.

But the three terms I spent at this all-consuming task as national board member of a federation of an Olympic sport turned me into an adult.

It was hard. I had to pay attention. Because I was now responsible and there were minutes of public record [*Celeste was appointed secretary in July 2005*]. I had to know all angles of the sport of triathlon, backwards and forwards. I had to understand. I had to ask questions. I soon learned that most of the questions I asked were questions the rest of the men had but were too proud to ask. "Explain it to me like I was six years old," became my *leitmotif*. My Schtick was that of the Old Woman who … asked.

So I learned a lot. I learned about politics, how men will sell their own mothers to promote themselves; that things happen because someone will benefit; and that few people in a company or in our country act for the good of all. I was stunned.

I learned how to be the type of woman a man would listen to. First off, I had what they would call "historical perspective." I walked the walk. I was able to get through to the men. Maybe because I had an aggressive type A husband and knew how to talk to them. You see they have a need for power. There was a lot of power play. And I always said what I mean to say. There is not a lot of curtain to pull back to see who I am.

I am most proud of learning to stand up for what I believed, even though I was the only one in the room with such a vote. And I have been proved right, actually. Triathlon taught me that just because he is a guy and has a you-know-what, does not mean that he has just put your wheel correctly on your bike. You need to check his work.

And so I learned not to be the sum total of the last thing said to me. I learned to think for myself. Triathlon had taught me who I was. And who I was, was not who my husband was. No one stood behind me to bolder up what I would say. I stood there alone. Just as I stood alone on the beach at the start of a triathlon.

To men readers, to young women readers—the above may sound somewhat a little naff. But remember, I was a woman whose husband had told her she did not have to go to the bathroom, whose parents told her, no, she was not sick—unless she threw up in the kitchen.

I liked being on the board. I liked the deferment. I have to say I got swallowed up in the position of power. It was addictive. I loved it. I loved the respect. I loved the purity of doing what I thought was the right thing to do, when I had the only knowledge in the room of how things had been done.

But it was a six-year 25 hour a week volunteer job, with, as the men say, your nuts on the table.

I got discouraged toward the end of my terms. I could see that the men were using the ersatz importance of their self-appointed governing roles to fill in for a daytime life that did not contain a pedestal. I think I knew I was done when one of the presidents of the board, on the evening of his election for same, said: "This is the happiest day of my life."

I was hoping I had not yet had mine.

I learned that men still have a journey still to make. We women fought valiantly for our rights, and we appreciate what we have. Men feel entitled, particularly men over the age, now in 2020, of fifty-five. I was surprised at the political antics sprouted from greed and the need for power that came from grown men who should have had their hands slapped. We women are within reach of an equitable stance. Women's journeys are different to men and we need to find a place for men to begin as well. Or wait till the old guys die out.

Just as Dottie's language oscillates between the personal and collective when she writes about her first Ironman triathlon in 1985, so too Celeste's account of her triathlon committee work swings from single to plural and shifts from first person to second and third. In Dottie's account, the vibrating tone of the narrative seems to pull both positions— the personal and collective—into the journey she is describing. Here, too, Celeste appears to equate her own trek with that of women—not just in triathlon, but also—more broadly. Reading Celeste's account of her committee work I feel that if she has something to say about the role women can play in shaping sporting cultures, it is that the process of change has barely begun.

Celeste's time on the USAT board of directors does not represent the end of her contribution to triathlon governance, but rather just another point of interest in the narrative landscape:

I was also involved in the International Triathlon Union (ITU) Age Group Commission. I found that extremely important because what is good for the goose is not always good for the gander. ITU is really for the pros, but it helps to say to cities, "We are going to bring in thousands of people and fill the hotels and restaurants." We do that so that a small group of pros can come in and perform. There were different rules for pros, and age groupers had to get off the course if they took too long. Age groupers would bring their problems to me. So I was involved in that.

I was also involved in Pan–American triathlon activities. I was the American representative because I speak Spanish. Sarah Springman from the ITU asked me and I wanted to help South American women. The women were oppressed. Triathlon is not for everybody. This is the sport for kids who have parents who can drive them everywhere. So they needed help.

In her memoir and my interviews with her, Celeste omits to mention other achievements or contributions to community undertaken while she metamorphosed from wife and mother, to athlete, and finally to advocate for female participation in sport. She says nothing about her philanthropic endeavors, such as those relating to the Denver Art Museum, and the Children's Museum of Denver. I wonder whether their absence is because they related to the wealth and influence Celeste acquired by marrying well. Celeste could perform such roles without confronting the expectations of parents, husband or social equals. Their absence from her memoir affirms that such activities have little to do with the final destination of the narrative trail. As she commented over dinner at Naples, she could gain "recognition through good grades and good deeds," but they did not make her "visible" for herself.

Other omissions from Celeste's memoir reinforce this point. I was stunned when Celeste let slip that her mother used to run. Somehow that surprising piece of information did not seem relevant to her. In the rosary she recites about her sporting life, parental figures, teachers, the church, society, culture and convention all impose the rules and structures that confined her, until her epiphany as a young restless mother of three.

Likewise, Celeste only hints at her minor success as a writer in her memoir. She suggests that writing offered her a chance to do something for herself, even while she remained constrained by convention. Writing does not figure initially as a tool for breaking the chains that bound her, for transforming and freeing herself. Yet, as she continued the metaphorical trek away from the designated patch of familial duty and pleasure for which she had been prepared as a child and young adult, Celeste's writing evolved as well. When asked, she explained:

In Minnesota I remember telling my husband I wanted to be a writer. And he said to get a *Readers' Digest*. There was a writing group. I was pregnant with my third child and learned to write through them. I got a job writing theater reviews for St Paul's Theater. I had a man from across the street accompany me with a camera, and then I thought I would take my own pictures. So I started doing magazine articles and freelancing.

I did an article for *Seventeen* magazine. This was when we moved to South Dakota. The name of the story was "If all your clothes were new." The editor had me re-work it so many times. I got $350. I thought I should not have spent so much time re-writing.

I asked Dick to give me a book idea. He said, "Let's say Indians want to buy their land back, and there's a love story, a person in love with an Indian." My rejection slip said it was too literary for that type of story. So after the New York Marathon I wrote a few chapters about Jan and me doing a marathon and gave it to my friend. She called me at the tennis club, and she said it was the funniest thing. I sent the chapters off and found an agent, sent them to her. She called me from New York. She loved it. She said that it "made me laugh and cry." She asked why the women stayed with these husbands, "why don't they have an affair?" I didn't want to do that.

But it gave me an idea of how to write a book. My husband says the funniest things and I wrote them down. I wrote another one that was excellent on a word processor. But I lost it. It was about a normal married couple, about my father. It was ... my thing.

In itself Celeste's literary career remained a fairly minor affair. But possibly it gave her a healthy appreciation of the persuasive power of imagination and its creative forms. Around the same time that Celeste drafted the memoir she also decided to channel her philosophical and literary energies into a Master of Theology. I recall sitting at the kitchen table at Naples, with a cup containing the dregs of a morning coffee near my right hand, all my talking points exhausted, when a question about her thesis, posed out of curiosity, elicited a revealing response:

I have been interested in theology for some time, since I told a massage therapist that I don't understand redemption. I started doing courses about the Bible. As soon as we got back from London, I was invited to join a group of women doing religious studies at Harvard. They would pay $5,000 and go to Harvard and hear speakers. I found that Catholics don't read the Bible, just the *Bulletin*. I was astounded because I come from a narrow Catholic background. I've been an observant Catholic going to church and all that.

I got accepted to do Masters. I didn't want more middle-aged white men telling me what to do. But decided I wanted to do it, looking at the Bible and the scriptures from a philosophical and historical standpoint. I thought that would give me something else to do outside sport. I did my thesis on redemption as an imaginative construct. People think, "Why did Judy get killed? Why did Jesus die?" Atonement theory is convoluted, but I learned that guilt is such a major thing in Christianity and the notion of redemption is a way of dealing with it.

Reflecting now—much later—on this analysis, I am struck by two things. First, Celeste's use of the term "imaginative construct" strengthens the point that her memoir narrative is sculpted with intent. It is not biographical. Second, I wonder whether the clues scattered throughout Celeste's various narratives—some designed for readers, some selected over time as Celeste sought to construct a meaningful narrative for herself—are not leading me on a metaphorical journey to somewhere else, but rather inwards.

Why did Celeste feel redemption watching CWW women cross the finish line of their first triathlon? Possibly leading other women out of the wilderness of convention alleviated some of the lingering guilt she felt about seeking and having a life of her own. Convention taught her to surrender her own identity for the sake of others. Sport taught her to put her interests first. CWW affirmed the value of sport as a transformative and enriching activity. Yet sitting on the national governing body of an Olympic sport, with men who sought and exerted the same form of power as those on whom she had been taught to depend, did not do that. Inspired by Judy, Celeste's metamorphosis into an enabler—a woman who saw sport as key to the growth and transformation of other women— appears to have alleviated her guilt and evoked a feeling of redemption, while the politics of governance did not.

Celeste's third metamorphosis appears to have germinated in the rich and supportive atmosphere fostered by the Masters in Motion collective and extended the benefits experienced by that collective to more and more women. It gave her access to structures of power within the sport, which, to her, seemed to be framed by and around the interests of men. But Celeste did not set out to bring about cultural change in the governance of triathlon. In contrast, Dottie did. In parallel to her athletic journey, Dottie regularly undertook campaigns aimed at addressing inadequacies in the provision of sport, health, medical and education services. As will be seen, her memoir reveals that this personal proclivity overlapped with her own affirmative experience of triathlon and the Masters in Motion collective. Instead of seeking directly to facilitate personal change, Dottie pursued institutional change.

10

Changing the Culture
of Things

Celeste evolved from the stressed athlete that Dottie witnessed pro-
tecting her space at a triathlon in the 1980s and arrived at a point where
the interests and needs of other women became meaningful because of a
radical, sport-induced transformation of her sense of self. From Dottie's
memoir, it seems that her work to advance the place of women in triath-
lon was meaningful for other reasons. Famed for her boundless energy
and informed by a hard-working Protestant ethic and an influential
maternal role model, Dottie took up myriad goodwill projects over time.
Sport and health feature in much of her unpaid work to improve the lives
of others.

Against this backdrop it is a little harder to discern the specific
meaning that Dottie attaches to her work relating to women in triathlon,
a task complicated further by her tendency to narrate simply what hap-
pened (in most instances) rather than reflect on how she felt. And the dis-
tance between each metaphorical landmark in Dottie's sketch of a busy,
active life often obscures the connections between them. It feels like the
scrub is crowding in on the narrative trail, and the clues are camouflaged
behind sprays of fresh, glossy leaves.

Like Celeste, Dottie chooses particular memories and presents
them in a specific order in order to construct a meaningful narrative. So
I return to Dottie's "dots," and look again at the way in which she joins
them. In chapter two of the original memoir draft Dottie moves straight
from the story of her first proper fun run—the 1977 women-only Bonne
Bell mini-marathon in Boston—to her participation in the 1996 Atlanta
Olympic Torch Relay.

Fast forward to 1996 and the Atlanta Olympics. One of the inspi-
rations for any fledging athlete or even an "Old Guard" wannabe is to
observe The Olympic Torch Relay. It was very exciting, and very hum-
bling, for me to be selected to carry the torch in 1996. It was not just

passing "the Torch" that day, but the anticipation building up to that day as well.

A feature of the day itself, as other Torch Bearers can attest, is the selection of participants, which represent every walk of life. The uniforms, the bands, the publicity, the P.R. is just mind-boggling. My most vivid memory is my husband and children all running along beside me from receiving to pass off. The downtown area I jogged through had all the school children out on the sidewalks waving American flags and holding their hand-made signs, which were heartfelt, genuinely honest, with young thoughts and misspellings. How

Due to her many and diverse community projects, Dottie (right) was invited to participate in the 1996 Olympic Torch Relay prior to the Atlanta Olympics (Dottie Dorion Collection).

refreshing. The memorabilia I received was exquisite and was dedicated to the nearby college so that others might have that inspiration.

Of course a great deal happened in the two decades between Dottie's initiation as a runner and her recognition as an Olympic Torch Bearer. But by presenting the two highlights one after the other Dottie flags that—like Celeste—she has not set out to write an autobiography.

Instead Dottie uses passing reference to aspects of a lifetime of community service and achievement to provide context and explanation to stories of relevance to the memoir, stories about women, masters women and the benefits of sport. This strategic use of seemingly unrelated aspects of her life story in the memoir draft is apparent when Dottie outlines her role in the spread of hospice care. At first it appears as a tangent, albeit an interesting one. Dottie backtracks from stories about the Masters in Motion era to a tale about her years as a nursing student:

When I was in nursing school in the 1950s we had to train in many required services and one of these was a medical unit where we cared for patients who had end of life illnesses. In those days, patients could stay in the hospital as long as needed. One particular patient was told she was getting better by her doctor each morning when he made rounds. We knew that each day she was getting weaker and weaker and in more pain. We could only follow doctor's orders and give pain medication every three hours. It became so depressing to try and take care of her and keep her spirits up that as students on the floor we drew straws to see who would take care of her each day. I felt guilty about doing that— to keep lying to a dying patient was very upsetting to me. I knew in my heart of hearts there had to be a better way.

In 1978 I went with a friend to hear a minister speak on Hospice and how dying patients could receive compassionate care, pain control and make their own plans for "End of Life Care." Twenty years after nursing the dying patient, I had an answer. The Rev. Paul Brenner and several like-minded friends banded together and founded Hospice of Northeast Florida. There were obstacles along the way, especially when the general public was calling it "Ho-Spice."

Three of us joined forces and went to the Florida State Capitol as lobbyists to change the original restrictive Hospice law, which required Hospices to own a hospital bed. This would have put all grass roots hospices—the very heart of the Hospice concept—out of business. We three—a retired Navy Captain, a mature lawyer/mother, and me, a nurse/special education teacher—invaded the legislature to correct this law. The Navy Captain persuaded the military and veterans to support us; the lovely, white-haired, lawyer lady used her Southern charms to arm twist; and me, well, I changed my clothes in front of the Capitol and literally chased down various legislators whose votes we needed. I must admit, I usually "Got My Man." The law was changed without one dissenting vote. We moved on to D.C. to encourage Hospice care to be covered through insurance reimbursement.

Directing this program was a challenge, besides caring for patients/ families all over the city. Just think, no cell phones, no computers, and eventually we went big time with beepers. Today, Hospice is a household word and millions of patients and their families are cared for by Hospice.

Dottie integrates these few paragraphs into her memoir in the context of her shock over Judy's death, making the point that nothing, not even her extensive experience in dealing with dying patients, could prepare her for that news. Possibly modesty prevents Dottie from elaborating further on what appears to be a significant contribution to the comfort and quality of life of terminally ill Americans. Possibly she is wary about devoting too much of the memoir to non-sporting aspects of her life. Preparing for my visit to Florida, I wondered what else she might say about hospice care if she was not trying to craft the story for inclusion in her memoir.

Sitting at the large dining room table at her home in Jacksonville, and surrounded by mounds of personal papers and records, I asked Dottie to tell me more. In contrast to the memoir, her verbal response is long and detailed. Briefly reminding me about "the woman dying of cancer" *that she encountered while nursing, Dottie elaborated a little more on her nursing career—in the process making the point that whether paid or unpaid, she always* "worked." *Resuming the hospice story with reference to her attendance at the 1978 Paul Brenner seminar, Dottie's account adds more color to the outline presented in her memoir draft:*

He talked about the origin of hospice. It came from England. When I heard him talk about it, a light went off in my head. He spoke about pain control, unlimited visiting hours, keeping patients in home with pets and kids, and all the specialists. I thought I finally found the answer, all those years later. So I got involved with Paul Brenner, Shirley Doyle, Gene Lewis and all these key people.

Brenner and Doyle had patients in their homes before people knew what we were doing. Then we started developing all the plans and the guidelines. We tried to educate ourselves. We set up a hospice program, with a desk and filing cabinet under the stairs at the Red Cross here. That's how we started. I was so excited. Paul was the father of Hospice of Northeast Florida and we started the program, setting the guidelines for it. We had a psychologist, a doctor and nurses and we really got involved with our patients in 1979.

We were not-for-profit, but a hospice started in a hospital here and at Sarasota, and Miami, where three entrepreneurs who saw potential for money-making set them up. They had lobbyists and they wrote the original hospice law. We knew something was going on, but we were so busy trying to survive. Then we found out the law they wrote was passed and it said that a hospice had to own a hospital bed. That destroyed the original concept of hospice and threatened to put all grass roots hospices out of business. We were a fledging organization and didn't have money. We recruited ministers, nurses, and doctors to do voluntary work.

We had to go to Tallahassee for a year to change the law. We had three people with diverse backgrounds and could get to every legislator and their key aids in Tallahassee as registered lobbyists. I'd pick the runners, and find out when they were running, and try to catch them and then run with them. We would work all the way on the drive up there and have a plan. I would plot a running course. It was kind of devious. We weren't professional lobbyists. And they knew we were right. Eventually it was passed, tacked on to another bill, without one dissenting vote. We pretty well laid out all the rules and regulations for the state.

But we knew it couldn't remain volunteer only. There were too many components, and volunteers burn out. We couldn't operate forever without being paid. In our first year of operation the budget was $500, and we didn't know where it would come from. We begged and borrowed. We made more trips to Tallahassee and then to Washington, D.C., and testified there that we needed to get hospice into the reimbursement system. They were receptive but we had to go through the red tape. They did get it into private insurance policies first, then Medicare.

Meanwhile our own program was growing. We had eight patients and moved into a doctor's examination room, with a little window way up the top. We wrote nursing notes sitting on the toilet. We thought we had arrived and started hiring people. But we faced other issues: doctors were very resistant, thinking we were stealing their patients.

Bit by bit all that changed. It was a really big struggle. We had AIDS patients, but one partner would die and the other was left alone. And a husband would die, and the wife would be left alone with no caregivers. We wanted to build a home for patients who didn't have caregivers so with a generous donation we built one. We moved to the Wells Complex and set up a board and employed more staff. People were becoming aware and were grateful for the help. We offered pain control, honesty, comfort, improved diet, and we educated families about the process of dying, instead of brushing it under the table. We helped them to prepare for funerals, set up wills, and to ease the minds of family members.

As a hospice nurse what continues to be so unbelievable is that every family took us in as one of their own. They trusted us. There are very few jobs where they trust you. That was the greatest privilege, and the rewards you have are so great. We did anything we could for them. We flew one family in. One man wanted to stay alive until Superbowl. Someone else wanted to see a grandchild, or someone getting married. There was one lady near the end of her life. She hadn't eaten for months. She wanted to go to a fast food place and have a hamburger, milkshake and fries, so we took her in her nightgown, dressing gown, and bunny slippers. We drove her to the fast food drive through. She had it, ate it all, happy as can be. Then the next day she died. You never forget one patient.

My husband was trained. He was working with this one particular patient, and the patient wanted to do a genealogy. They were all working on it. When my husband was away on a trip I called and told him that the patient died. He was upset because the genealogy was not finished. George had more things to add. However, a son later finished the job. In hospice you don't plan for the next day. You have to fulfill whatever wish on that day. George never did have another patient.

For a long time, we relied on grants and foundations and individual donations. One generous family donated money for the first Hadlow Center. We spent a lot of time planning that and got a very good architect. Every room looks out on a garden or trees. It has a kitchen, a room for music, a chapel, adequate parking, and lovely grounds. We even built it so people can bring their pets. There was opposition in the beginning, because they didn't want dead people in hearses going in and out all day. That was so far from the truth.

Hospice care is almost commonplace, but I think when it becomes commonplace, you lose the spirit and intent of hospices. Everyone either knows of it or has used it. The core group never ever wavered in thinking this was the right thing to do. But it was exhausting. We were seeing people all over three counties day and night. It was very hard on my family. We got beepers. It was hard in the middle of the night. Sometimes I hadn't slept for days. I stuck with it as long as I could. It was a very important part of my life. I would never change it or the people I was working with. It's so satisfying. People say, "How can you do that?" I just want to make the end game better.

Dottie did not single-handedly bring hospice care into being, but in early 1982, the board of the Hospice of North East Florida sent her a letter of gratitude, preserved with appreciation in Dottie's papers. The contents of the letter clearly demonstrate the extent to which she devoted herself to the cause and contributed to its foundation and consolidation. Struggling for superlatives, the vice president of the board wrote:

Beyond Triathlon

You have defied the laws of biology in your Hospice service. Heretofore, the human being was believed to be incapable of the kind of mental, spiritual and physical exertion you have shown. Not only have you kept the Hospice heart beating vigorously, but your unlimited enthusiasm and commitment have been an inspiration to us all. To say, "We couldn't have done it without you," is understating it by a mile.

Yet the memoir provides only enough information to flag that Dottie was involved in the campaign to establish the hospice concept. It does not—nor is it meant to—demonstrate the full extent of the commitment, enthusiasm and compassion that she poured into the cause.

The same is true of Dottie's references in the memoir to other areas of paid and unpaid work, such as special education, and free medical clinics. Like the hospice anecdote, Dottie slips comment about her work in the field of learning disabilities into the memoir narrative about her transformation into a runner. In that instance a camp for children with various related conditions, at which she was compelled to sprint after a rogue child, represented a first public demonstration of her newly acquired skills as a runner.

When I met Dottie at her Jacksonville home, "special education" was the next talking point on my list after "hospice." Looking back at the transcript of that session it seems curious that, when prompted, she offers more detail, though in a less passionate and engrossed manner than her lengthy elaboration on the Hospice campaign:

I started at the University of North Florida [UNF] in 1971. It was founded in '69 and wasn't even at the location it is now. I was there when it had one building and a dirt road. I went to UNF for certification in Special Education teaching. I spent a decade while I was nursing and raising children in Connecticut studying for a Master of Special Education, but what I had was not adequate. I found the UNF Certificate pretty easy.

As a special education teacher, I ran a school for children with learning disabilities. But I felt that in summer kids had nothing but TV, so decided to establish a camp for them. It was especially for children with learning disabilities, such as short attention span and so on. I established an association and got about forty volunteers and went to a private school and used their facilities in the summer.

I had a grant and gave them good lunches, and healthy snacks. We did stories and reading, plays, art, and swimming. I tried to expose them to different things as much as we could but kept things short and fun because they didn't have the attention span. They would shoot baskets and try to work out the percentages. We did have time out and pulled them out of activities and settled them down a bit. After a couple of weeks, they felt like they could do anything. We still keep in touch with some kids from the camp. It was a very, very good learning opportunity and it gave a lot of the kids exposure to a lot of things.

While discussing her work for children with learning disabilities, Dottie made a significant statement about the driving principle behind much of her work:

When I arrived here it was so Old South. It was a big, big step back. There was so much segregation. There was a maid's bus that would come here and drop all the maids off. There was one road and twenty houses. There was a golf course and rinky-dink clubhouse.

All of us have to change the culture of things in order to accomplish the things we want and the things we are trained to do. I took advantage of opportunities because many of the Southern women were not working professionally. Many of their days were spent in what I might consider frivolous activities: shopping, beauty parlors, and dressing for parties. This gave me many opportunities I might not have had elsewhere. I could pick and choose opportunities and challenges, which were needs not being fulfilled.

The phrase that stands out to me is "change the culture of things." It seems to ring true for the hospice campaign, Dottie's work for children with learning disabilities, and also her slightly more recent efforts to address the inequalities embedded in the American health care system through an organization called Volunteers in Medicine.

Over a decade ago a local doctor and I founded a free medical clinic for the working uninsured in our community. For years I did kayak for a charity event at Hilton Head. I did that with a friend of mine. We started early in the morning and kayaked all day. It was a wonderful opportunity to talk. I didn't know what the Charity was and at the dinner I found out it was for Volunteers in Medicine. It was started by Dr. Jack McConnell, who lived in Hilton Head. He was out driving and picked up someone hitch hiking. When he asked the hiker, "What do you do for medical care?" the man replied, "I wish I had medical care." Dr. McConnell decided he would found a free medical clinic especially for those on the island. He started small and it became bigger. I met him and talked to him some more and thought that makes sense.

About six months later I went to a dinner and fund raiser. When I was there, I met Dr. Jim Burt. I asked what he was doing now that he was retired, and he said some sort of missionary work, or giving back to the community. I told him about Volunteers In Medicine. He talked to McConnell and got back to me and said he would like to do it here.

We needed volunteer doctors and nurses, and we needed a place. We found an old deserted building in inner city Jacksonville. There were holes in the roof and rain pouring through. It was pretty well collapsed, but it had two stories, was on a corner, and had parking, which was good because it was on a main street. It took a lot of work to restore. So we went out and had a board set up with warm bodies. We had a doctor who contacted other doctors. We congregated at a church and one man came wheeling in, in his wheelchair. He said, "I owe a debt to society and I'm going to oversee construction." Then another person had connections with a decorator. All the puzzle pieces fell into place. Then we found someone in the flooring business, and the decorator said, "If you do solid flooring, I can do some carpets." Hospitals donated tables, and equipment that was not being used any more. We got filing cabinets, desks, and chairs from companies going out of business. They just wanted to get rid of it, not to make money.

Anytime someone was getting rid of something it came to us. Someone called up and said they had paint and came down on the Easter weekend and painted the building. On Easter Sunday we were driving to St John's Cathedral—a church downtown—and my husband said, "Well you've got your Easter egg!" It was painted the brightest blue with lots of other colors. It wasn't exactly what I was looking for, but everyone can find it.

The stairs were redone. We put most of the offices and a conference room upstairs and a very nice break room and kitchen downstairs. We built the exam rooms, a very nice foyer, a children's room, and a waiting room. We had our symbol in tiles on the floor—a wonderful heart. One Thursday I said, "We're just missing a rocking chair." On Friday I went to work, and it was there. Then we set up a pharmacy and got free medication, or heavily discounted short-dated medications.

So we got it up and running, and I was out on the sidewalk pulling people in. We felt that the working uninsured were the most neglected. They fell through the cracks. I was asking questions for their forms and I never heard so many stories in my life. And I know they weren't making them up because you wouldn't make these stories up.

I remember all of them, but one woman in particular came in and said she had a lump in her breast, and she had a lump that was the size of a golf ball. You almost feel like crying because you think, "How long have you had this problem?" I reassured her and asked, "Why didn't you get this seen to before?" She said she went to the hospital three days in a row and never got called up. She went back to work on the fourth day and her boss said, "If you go today, you'll be fired!" We had all her tests done in one day on Tuesday, and on Friday we had her at the Mayo Clinic getting treatment for breast cancer.

We set up clinics at night and office hours on Saturdays, because that's when people had time off. We had some specialists. We had eye exams, and treated diabetics. We also set up free dental care, partnering with a center downtown with all the equipment and a volunteer dentist. The patients would go over for their dental work. So many of them had systemic infections.

Emphasis is placed not only on the treatment of disease, but also the prevention of disease. Half our problem is obesity. We partner with UNF and have nutrition students that deal with diet problems. We had students set up programs with pedometers to measure exercise, and psychological professionals to address mental health issues. Whatever we can't be, we try to partner with someone who can. It's been a very successful program.

We get very good publicity in newspapers and on television and were able to get very good donors and grants. We have had the Women with Heart event, and other dinners, and running teams to raise funds. That's what kept the program running. Today there are over ninety *Volunteers in Medicine Clinics* in the U.S.

This detailed account about Volunteers in Medicine tells me a lot about the way that Dottie works: to "change the culture of things" she looks for sustainable mechanisms. Leveraging her networks as well as the knowledge and resources of like-minded communities across the city, state and country she pursues legislative reform, education and innovation, and attempts to foster cultural adaptation within target groups to promote improved health.

Advocating exercise as a way to improve the health and quality of life of disadvantaged groups, Dottie became involved in yet another cause—Community Connections:

I served for eight years on the board of an organization that originated with the YMCA [Y], and then became Community Connections. It was a three-story building, which became home for homeless women and their children.

I thought there was a crying need for a fitness program to meet the obvious needs of overweight women and children and their related medical conditions. I discussed it with the board and decided they

161

In 2002 Dottie co-founded the Volunteers in Medicine Jacksonville Clinic, pictured here with fellow founder Dr. James Burt at the clinic launch in 2003 (courtesy Bob Self and *Florida Times-Union*).

should have a workout room in the basement with basic equipment. We set up numerous programs to address their diet and exercise.

In some ways I felt that I failed with the women. I couldn't motivate them. It was really hard to get the women to do exercise because they worked. There were some successes and many trials and errors, too. We started a yoga program in the evenings. Music was especially motivational for these women to exercise and when we played a Gospel Aerobics tape, we definitely "Hit a home run." It was so popular that the children started coming with the Moms to participate. The kids were enthusiastic and very teachable. This inspired us to start a kids' karate program.

We never lost sight of our goals and we invented every way we could to motivate these women to healthier lifestyles. We played games, we brought in chefs to teach healthy cooking, we showed all kinds of tapes to inspire, and we organized teams to practice healthy food preparation. When we first served healthy food platters after workouts, it was ignored but over time it improved. The children were more receptive.

All in all, plans would progress, but if I left, everything regressed back to the old ways. I would come back and they were right where we began, and they were trying to hide their stomachs. They had to have some will power on their own and keep doing things.

The participants would say, "Miss Dottie, we learn so much from you." And I would respond, "Oh, no, I learn more from you than you ever learn from me." One example is a rewards program I started, based on the completion of workouts. The rewards were not tee shirts, water bottles, or some usual gift. When fifteen workouts had been officially completed, they got a free bus pass. (I wanted them to walk, but many had to bus to work.) When twenty-five workouts were completed, they got a $25 gift certificate to a grocery store. We had no reward in the event that fifty workouts were completed. It was probably unrealistic. But I had them get together and decide what the reward would be. Sometimes I think I am too old to be amazed by something new. Here was a reward I would never have dreamed of in a million years.... "tattoo removal!" Think about it.

I trained them enough to do a race in the city. We had medical students doing evaluations on all the participants and when they were deemed ready, we took them on the local 5K walk/run event. "Our" participants were all given red caps to wear so I could keep track of them. I was running back and forwards checking them, but then one woman suddenly disappeared. She'd be down at the landing with some guy.

One night a resident woman came in to work out on a bike, but she didn't have sneakers on. I asked her "Please put on your shoes as it could be dangerous on the bike." She said, "Well, I can't because these are my son's shoes and we have to share them." Thus began the quest for more shoes. All sporting goods stores were visited in person and frequently. When they got sick of me "begging" they would just take me to the back storage room of sales and say, "Just take what you need." (And, not spoken but understood, please don't come back!) The women were so happy to receive their gift shoes all wrapped up and tied with a red ribbon. However, "No good deed goes unpunished." When one woman received a running shoe with a "Swoosh," everyone wanted a shoe with a Swoosh.

Sadly, Community Connections closed due to financial difficulties. Maybe the kids remember having a good time there. It was a nice place to play and do karate classes. I hope maybe it touched their lives.

Naturally Dottie hoped that Community Connections had a lasting personal impact on the values and behaviors of the individuals for whom the service was intended. While her efforts were well intended, it seems that she struggled to "change the culture of things" in the case of the disadvantaged women and children of Jacksonville. It is probable that the cultural change needed in the case of Community Connections, entailed more than temporary access to sporting facilities and opportunities.

Dottie enacted the same belief in the value of active and healthy lifestyles in many other schemes to reach and positively impact various groups of people:

Another desire of mine, because I worked with kids with learning and other disabilities, I really wanted to see physically challenged athletes get into [*Jacksonville Track Club*] races. Bob Hall was the first one I met personally. He made his own chair and he was prepared to race. I got him into the first River Run and he stayed with us. I really wanted to see him get into more races and approached Dave McGillivray who organized the Boston marathon and other charity events. I was also determined to get him into the New York marathon with Fred Lebow, but it was difficult because people were worried about accidents, and they hadn't worked out how to solve that.

One event I was pleased to be a part of was the kids' triathlon. Most of these came through the Y. They started and promoted it, and then the University got involved. It was so different. I couldn't believe these little kids were on their bikes, some trained by the Y and other clubs or schools. I couldn't believe how well behaved they were and what good sportspeople they were. They loved it. I was standing there all day putting medals around their neck and seeing their joy and their pride. I couldn't wait for the next one. If you make it manageable for all those kids, you can make it successful. You feel so good because you started something.

At UNF we did a lot of programs that I was instrumental in. Tiger Holmes, together with many volunteer swimmers started, "Every Child a Swimmer." [*This was the program Dottie mentioned when she briefly mentioned participating in the 1988 Masters World Swimming Championships.*] We had witnessed a high number of child drownings every year—kids grew up and got to high school and were too embarrassed to say they didn't know how to swim. We taught them to swim, to float, and how to save a life. It was a great program and we're trying to bring that back. A couple of years ago the University took out the swimming pool since it needed significant repairs. Now we have a project for a pool in the City. We had our Masters Swimming using the University pool but now it is gone and they've installed basketball courts.

Dottie also set out to "change the culture" in an area that related directly to her own experiences as a pre–Title IX woman with natural sporting talents and a competitive spirit. Just over a year after competing in the 1977 Bonne Bell mini-marathon she pushed for a women-only running event in Jacksonville. A race report in Dottie's collection of memorabilia reveals that the 800-odd women who participated in the first Natural Light Women's 5000 caught sponsors by surprise—they ran out of competitor tee shirts. It seems that Dottie was not alone in her desire for the opportunity to run with other women.

The race represented just a starting point for Dottie's prolonged and multifaceted campaign to improve sporting opportunities for women, but in her memoir, she takes the time to contextualize her efforts in terms of broader campaigns:

The Title IX legislation in the U.S. required a really concerted effort from women and men to create equality for women in sports. There was steady progress but not withstanding there was still strong opposition, reluctance, and many obstacles to overcome. Kathryn Switzer's "illegal" Boston Marathon in 1967 led to eventual inclusion of women to that race in 1972. Then, our heroine, Joan Benoit Samuelson, won the first ever women's marathon gold medal in the 1984 Olympics. These pioneers, and many more, paved the way for women's participation in a lot of sports. Organizations to foster equality for women emerged: the Women's Sports Foundation and many other women's committees. One aim is board representation in athletic programs at every education level. There is always more work to be done and vigilant overseers to maintain and enforce Title IX.

The next sentence in Dottie's memoir offers a signpost that re-directs her readers from a fairly well-known thoroughfare in narratives of change in women's sport, back onto her own path. It seems to encapsulate the leitmotif emerging within her memoir:

A change at the local grassroots level is where we can make the biggest difference for equality in women's sports.

As with Dottie's references to her work in hospice care, special education, and community health care, the memoir account she provides regarding her pursuit of equal sporting opportunities for women and men at UNF, is relatively limited. Dottie makes many assumptions when she connects the dots, making it difficult for the reader to follow. After prodding her for more details, I found the narrative trail in her memoir a little easier to follow.

Brought together, it seems that the timing of Dottie's arrival in Jacksonville shortly after the foundation of the University of North Florida

*presented her with a chance to shape sporting culture at the grass roots
level, by intervening in the policies and practices of the tertiary institu-
tion. Despite her persistent effort, cultures of inequality proved resilient
and difficult to change. As the verbal and written accounts interwoven in
the following narrative reveals, Dottie's efforts to ensure that a culture of
gender equity characterized the health and sport offerings of the fledgling
university meant that she joined with a movement to "change the culture"
of sport that was simultaneously enacted by myriad women, individually
and collectively, across the nation.*

Many "moons" ago the local University where I live had a major
problem in providing equality for women in sport. At least, that is what
I strongly believed.

The University just had one building when I got there. It was the
wild, wild west with deer and alligators, and boar pigs.

Tennis, the first sports program there, was established in the early
1980s. We had a tennis team but no courts. Determination was our
game. We went out and raised money from companies and named the
courts after the donors. One was named after a car company, etc. So we
built tennis courts and won a championship in our first year.

The challenge for women's teams began as soon as the sports programs were initiated. The training room was a closet with bare bones—
just three pieces of equipment. The trainer pulled a little red wagon with
supplies and food. At matches I would cut up oranges and take them
out. I recently met someone on the first tennis team, and she remembered those oranges.

The men on teams had uniforms, traveled on buses, and had a food
allowance. The women drove their own cars (with no gas allowance),
stayed in the homes of opposing team members, and brought their own
food or paid for it with their own money. We passed the hat to get funds
for them to travel to each event.

When the newly formed Varsity Club was established in 1982, I was
the "token" woman on the board. The only reason I was asked is because
my husband had declined.

The first Varsity Club board meeting was in a tiny conference room.
It was all men. I was the only woman. We started going around the table
to get office bearers. Of course, they all pointed at me and took it for
granted that I would be Secretary. I stood up and pounded my fist on the
table and said, "I will never be secretary." Then I stood up on my "Soap-
box" and gave them an earful. I gave a lecture saying that when you're
secretary of an organization, it stops you from contributing because

you're just taking notes. I said, "If you want a Secretary hire one, get a tape recorder, or you men do the job." So I got strong and stood up for myself. And I just rebelled against it. One board member looked at me and shook his head and later said, "I knew we had somebody who would be a mover and shaker." I was never taken for a "token" afterwards and eventually they granted me the respect I deserved.

Documents in the UNF and Florida State Archives reveal that within three years, Dottie was nominated as the Varsity Club (which shortly afterward was re-named the Osprey Club) President. Its central function was to raise funds in support of sport and athletics at the University. Dottie resigned as President in December 1989 in order to highlight "existing problems," *including mismanagement of Osprey Club and endowment funds. However, her concerns about the management of sport and athletics at the University persisted. A state review of compliance across Floridian education institutions commenced in 1990 and reported that UNF recorded the lowest rate of female participation in sports. With state funds at risk, UNF was urged to address gender inequity in scholarship offerings, sports programs and facilities.*

In conversation, Dottie added to a very brief comment in her memoir about her work to address these issues:

Around 1972 we heard about Title IX. [*In 1990*] I got together with another woman—Dr. Betty Flinchum—at UNF. She did a lot of good work. She did a lot of international work, for study abroad students. We got together when we heard about Title IX. The Governor had appointed various committees and we were a bit left out and decided to do something about it, with other women. In conjunction, we set up a scholarship program for women. The University was paying $12,500 and we were getting the match for all of those to make them $25,000 each.

Then we got more involved; we were in communication with someone in Tallahassee and kept in communication to see what was going on with compliance. UNF had hired an Athletic Director who was really out of line. I got details on him. I knew we had tennis and cross country slowly developing as sports programs. We added three or four sports programs and didn't have money for them. I started documenting women's programs versus men's sports programs. I kept getting evidence everywhere.

It took two years with the cooperation of several other supporters to get the documentation on the Athletic Director, who was eventually fired. They have a compliance officer now. "The Wheels of Progress Move Slowly but Surely!"

Removal of the Athletic Director represented a step toward compliance, but the women's teams still suffered from inferior facilities and funding. UNF archival records show that Dottie made a substantial personal contribution to enable the renovation of the Osprey Club Fitness Center to include women's showers, a locker room and other equipment and resources. In recognition of her contribution, the state legislature approved an application in 1995 to rename the building in Dottie's honor. Dottie does refer to the Center in her memoir:

Today the original Dottie Dorion Fitness Center has grown like "Topsy" to The Student Wellness Complex. Now, the second floor is The Dottie S. Dorion Fitness Center. Students see me today and ask, "Are you really Dottie Dorion?" You see—if a building is named for someone usually the person is dead. The building has allowed all students, including the physically challenged, to utilize state of the art gym facilities. I love the smoothie bar and the climbing wall! We are so grateful for all the students and donors who helped make this fitness center possible. The athletes have taken advantage of coaches and trainers to elevate their competitive sports to become a fully fledged athletic program in NCAA Division 1.

Dottie's delight at the impact of her efforts is apparent. In her memoir she expresses satisfaction about other contributions to the sporting life of the University and the health and progress of its students:

All of these opportunities inspired us—my husband and I—to make opportunities available to other potential participants by dedicating endowed scholarships at several colleges in the area of sports, health and ecology. How rewarding to be "stewards" of future successes.

In conversation Dottie explained a little more about these contributions, but she does so in the context of making a core point about her work at the University:

My take home message is to get more women involved on Boards. Men are more likely to get involved and they do that for business reasons. We did a lot from the Varsity Club to the Osprey Club. It's grown now to have all the components of a Health College. We've also been very involved in the health college there, setting up endowed athletic and nursing scholarships and a simulation lab. I received many nice honors at UNF. I was the first woman in the Athletics Hall of Fame. I hope over there I've been a role model on boards and search committees. I hope I have shown what I have been able to do financially and as an athlete, so people can get "off their duff" and get out there. I'm very proud of how the Brooks Health College has progressed. Hopefully we will see more women as Athletic Directors and Coaches. It makes me mad when they hire a man for the women's team when a coach leaves. We have and need to train for women to do things like that. I hope to have input.

Dottie may have donated much-needed funds to the University in a calculated manner. But the implied point in her memoir—and one that comes out more firmly in her verbal account—is that through her participation on a variety of Boards, by daring to act in a context in which women were expected to follow passively, she contributed to lasting "change in the culture of things" at the University.

By the early-to-mid 1990s, Dottie had lobbied state and federal politicians for reform to legislation regarding the hospice concept. She had drawn on Jacksonville networks to foster local hospice services and played a role in early Jacksonville Track Club activities, particularly those aimed at involving disadvantaged groups in the sport of running. Recognition for her hospice work came largely from within the hospice movement, and as a result of the linkages between the board members and the metropolitan newspaper The Florida Union-Times. *That recognition contributed to Dottie's nomination for the 1982 Eve Award for service to the community. She was also inducted into the Jacksonville Track Club Hall of Fame. But—alluding to the original memoir title "Contents May Have Shifted" and the metaphor of airplane travel—Dottie concludes the section about her work at UNF, with the following words:*

"Taxiing" from the secure jetway and "running" to the unknown gives heebie-jeebies.

The implication seems to be that Dottie's work on the Board of the Varsity Club, and to prevent the institutionalization of gender inequality in University Sports Programs, proved more daunting than most of her efforts to "change the culture of things." To achieve her aims she ventured into "unknown" territory, a space in which she felt less "secure." Once more Dottie seems to suggest that vulnerability is intrinsic to the pursuit of change.

It is possible that this is also true of her wish to organize the inaugural masters women's breakfast at the 1991 ITU Triathlon World Championships in Australia. In 1991, Dottie faced two unknowns, her first Triathlon World Championships, and her challenge to a male figure of power at UNF. Was it a feeling of vulnerability and a need for the fortifying company of others like her that made the idea of reproducing the protective and enabling tradition of the women's breakfast at the ITU world championships appealing?

As it was—just as Celeste's work with CWW aligned with the aims of the USAT Board—Dottie's wish to offer encouragement and support to masters women triathletes at the "Worlds" aligned with the ideals espoused by key ITU figures. A short, typed document in Dottie's collection affirms that the ITU congress passed a motion to establish a Women's Commission [ITUWC] in 1990. The ITUWC planned gatherings for women at the 1990 Triathlon World Championships in Orlando, and again for the 1991 Championships on the Gold Coast. Unaware of this development, Dottie's breakfast diverted part of the intended audience from Women's Commission events. The breakfast also clashed with an ITUWC event scheduled prior to the 1992 world championships in Edmonton, Canada. Finally, at the 1993 World Championships in Manchester, Dr. Sarah Springman from the United Kingdom, and Dr. Lori Cameron from Australia—both of whom generated much of the early energy within the ITUWC—approached Dottie and asked her to join them.

Writing about her work with the Commission Dottie presents a selective overview and limited sense of chronology, quotes Women's Commission documentation regarding its aims, and provides the reader with some intriguing anecdotes:

It seems eons ago that The International Triathlon Union Women's Commission was started and believe it or not, it was a man who really got it off the ground. "Talk is cheap" and "Action speaks louder than words," so around 1989–90 Les McDonald, the Canadian President of the ITU, selected the Women's Commission co-chairs. Dr. Sarah Springman of Britain laid out the role of the Women's Commission and wrote the action plan and with McDonald's leadership and persuasion, sometimes strong arm, national federations were urged to send women to the ITU Congress.

The original goals of the Women's Commission, in order to become a full Board Committee, were: to ensure equality of opportunity, recognition and reward of women in triathlon; to increase the number of women taking part in triathlon at all levels; to assist in the development of triathlon worldwide; to have every region represented on the ITU Women's Committee and supporting the goals of This Committee, and to Monitor and evaluate our progress. These goals sounded quite far-fetched to me, knowing that we were barely at the starting line. When I heard all these goals, I half jokingly asked one of the leaders from Australia, Lori Cameron, "What will happen when we accomplish all these goals?" She replied, "When we accomplish all our original goals we can disband."

10. Changing the Culture of Things

These goals were passed by the ITU Congress in 1990 and backed with financial support. There were many supporters because, honestly, the women had nothing in this fledging sport, and had been treated as second-rate athletes. Not only that, they had more difficulties training with the lack of coaches for females, no financial endorsements and safety issues with training alone. This is not unlike other sports in the beginning.

Despite its early commitment to gender equality, Dottie identifies the ITU Congress as the source of many of the obstacles encountered by the Women's Commission, and a key target of many original schemes:

In Congress the men had multiple awards, the women few; the National Federation attendees at Congress were 90 percent men, and equality for women in education initiatives in both athlete and coach development needed to get on a level "Playing Field." We firmly believed that we must achieve these goals in English speaking countries if we were to be successful down the road in other parts of the world.

"Never mess with women on a Mission." Efficient communication was essential and thus was born, The International Triathlon Union *Newsletter*. This was essential to connect with the eleven members of The Commission from all over the world. Our Board Representative, Lise Jahnsen from Denmark, helped in innumerable ways. I don't like to sound like "Pollyanna," but we all worked together, and our chain had no weak link. Occasionally, communication took a little longer because sign language was used to bridge difficulties with unknown foreign languages. I still, to this day, consider this was what I call a David and Goliath situation. We mailed and faxed "our" newsletter, no easy task. Many Committee members are still treasured friends. Perhaps, when working closely with each other in what we considered a crisis, we became best friends. Today, Lise and her triathlete husband, who directed the ITU medical committee then, are two of our best friends and we share visits with them.

Congress presented our ultimate challenge to ingenuity so we, of course, rose to the occasion. There were a few, maybe many, tactics we used which were unusual and creative. Since Congress was predominately made up of men, we had to develop a strategy when it came to getting Resolutions passed. This may not have been on the "Up and Up" but it did work. I am not suggesting other groups do this and perhaps it is really old school now in the age of technology. The ITU Women's Commission became a Committee and proposed Resolutions every year. All of us went in person to lobby men from other countries whom we knew

171

were chauvinists and who would oppose us. So we would plot and plan to bring up "Our" Resolutions just before lunch. Usually Congress ran late, and participants were hungry and tired. They would pass any legislation just to get it over and go out to lunch. Next, we found in the afternoon, just after a heavy lunch, one of our main opposition groups would be not only sleepy from jet lag but also drowsy after the meal. Bingo! We could pass any resolution while they slept, and sometimes snored.

One tactic was called "the Brick and Flower" Ceremony. In Perth, Australia in 1997, I remember one particular ceremony. The presentation of a real brick went to the person(s) who were not supporting women's equality and actually continued to discriminate against women in triathlon. Now, how would you like to carry that prize back in your suitcase and explain it to your spouse? The flowers were presented to those who assisted, promoted and implemented equality for women. I can tell you there were some very surprised recipients. I keep thinking Washington, D.C., here in The States, just might be ready for this Ceremony.

Sometimes, I think I must have been naïve and the same of others. We always thought we would all be successful in fulfilling our goals and we did. However, along the way we did so much more than we ever dreamed possible. More possibilities just jumped in our way and I have always believed that "If you are doing the right things for the right reason, it will be successful."

One, just one, of the shining star programs of this Committee was a program we named "Adopt a Triathlete." This was to focus on three main countries we could assist with triathlon. We "Adopted" Bolivia because they had a very determined leader for developing triathlon for children. They were very limited in equipment and supplies and this was particularly true for bicycles. Children shared bikes since there weren't enough to go around. At races it was quite a spectacle, as one biker would come into the transition area and hand off his/her bike to another competitor. In order to be quick, the bike numbers of each competitor were attached to the bars and they would just flip the card for the next rider. Swimming was another challenge—just to find a pool for the swim portion. We sent swim goggles for them and this was a new and novel invention they had never heard of.

This whole process necessitated a sort of underground transportation system for sending needed supplies. Goods would be packaged up, shipped to a transfer person in Miami and the triathlon leader would pick them up and take them on to Bolivia. Just remember, "Where There's a Will, There's a Way."

10. Changing the Culture of Things

We had a wonderful contact in South Africa and decided they really needed assistance in this developing country. Thus, was born the "Adopt a Triathlete" in Africa. This program grew like "Topsy." My husband, while very supportive of these efforts, would no longer travel with me since I was transporting bikes in bike cases and not only bikes, but loaded to the hilt with other "tri" equipment (shoes, books, goggles, bike parts, and clothes).

When I was selected to give a paper at the Women in Sports Conference in Namibia, George declined to go with me. He did say if he wanted to see the animals he would go to a zoo, when I encouraged him to accompany me on a photographic safari. I believe he thought I would surely end up in jail and one in jail was better than two. Somehow, I did get through Customs with two full bike cases. Actually, I talked so fast to the agents with my non-stop chatter and they just said, "Go on." The bikes traveled from Province to Province each day to give more kids the opportunity to cycle. At night the bikes often found a safe haven locked up in a jail so they wouldn't be stolen. This program morphed into other programs and traveled to other countries.

I met a wonderful family in South Africa and the son was an aspiring triathlete. Their main need was for running shoes. Although I took off my own shoes and gave them to him, I assured him when I returned to The States, I would send him fifty pairs. When I returned, the quest for running shoes began. I went to all the running stores, track clubs and friends to get the fifty pairs of running shoes. The generosity was overwhelming.

Dottie's outline of her work to foster the increased global participation of women and children in the sport of triathlon omits a key moment of self-awareness. One experience in Africa led her to recognize the potentially irrelevant direction of ITUWC campaigns to reach women in developing countries. The epiphany struck a day before Dottie was scheduled to present at what she refers to as the "Women in Sports Conference in Namibia," the second International Women's Group World Conference on Women and Sport, held in 1998. Toward the end of a long day of interviews with Dottie, I raised the topic—mentioned only fleetingly in her memoir:

That was my trip to Africa in 1998. This was where I had to prepare my talk early so that it could be translated. And then I had lunch with three women from different parts of Africa. We had Kiwi stew. They were all eating with their hands. We had bread. One spoke French; others spoke different African dialects. None of us understood in languages but we still communicated. I started finding out what the problems were, and the problems were enormous.

I have had the privilege of speaking to a lot of different organizations. I don't believe in cookie cutter speeches. No matter whom, I want it to be appropriate. I really want to direct to their interest, organization, what they do, stress the positives of what they do. I always think about it before I give a speech and try and have some take home message. Sometimes I have quotes and sometimes my favorite sayings. I think it's really important.

At Namibia, I started out with originally talking about day care and corporate sponsorship. I had written the most erudite speech, and I said to my roommate from the ITU, "I cannot give this speech—it's pie in the sky." I re-wrote the speech, talking about the realities of feeding the children before they come, sharing the bikes, locking the bikes up in jails. Then I talked how we could help and teach them at home; give them exercises. The translators were livid. But I wasn't going to waste my time and their time. I really went at it. It was well received. Except a woman from France who was very unhappy. It was a good lesson. We take for granted their lifestyles are our lifestyles. We're at different ends

Dottie (right) with Mali Manga at the 1998 International Women's Group World Conference on Women and Sport, Namibia (courtesy Liesbeth Stoltz).

of the bell curve. The women work much harder than men and run the households.

There is no natural conclusion to the narratives of Dottie's efforts to involve more women—from Jacksonville to Bolivia to the world—in triathlon. There are some successes, but not the same tone of accomplishment that infuse her accounts of, say, the hospice campaign. Nor is there the sense of finality tinged with regret over goals not reached, as found in Dottie's account of Community Connections. Dottie's efforts to "change the culture" of women's sport, particularly triathlon, appear to focus on change at the grass roots with a view to enabling broader change. In the absence of a sense of completion, her accounts seem to suggest that the desired change has not yet occurred, or at the very least is not yet complete.

Reflecting on the narratives that Dottie and Celeste share about their "busy work," I wonder whether that is the point. While Dottie looked outward and Celeste looked inward, in many ways they sought the same thing. One pursued cultural change as it relates to women in sport through a personal process of mentoring and inspiration, and through it furthered her own personal confrontation of the gendered structures and expectations that previously constrained her, and others like her. The other pursued cultural change through structural and institutional means, bringing to her campaigns insights garnered from personal experience as well as observation of the realities confronting other women. One sought to transform individuals; the other sought to transform sporting structures. Both aims were radical. Neither, it seems, sought simply to improve women or sport. Rather they sought to produce something new.

But there is a sense in their memoirs that this "something new" is still in the making. Women's sport has not yet matured.

11

Crack Eggs, Not Bones

Against the backdrop of their respective campaigns to involve more women in triathlon and resisting conventional expectations that age would diminish their constructive participation in sport, Dottie and Celeste maintained active lives. In the process they put their bodies through a great deal. Describing the scenic features visible from their narrative trails through the forest of athletic adventure, neither traveler says much about her body even though—tamed and transformed— it enabled her journey and her metamorphosis into athlete and enabler. The silence provides another clue that the memoirs are not meant to be autobiographical.

In her memoir Dottie provides just an overview of the physical costs of her sporting adventures:

We understand the risks we take when we participate in sports. Or at least, we learned in a hurry. However, we didn't realize most of our body parts would be "Limited" at one time or another. That includes, but not limited to fractures, pulled muscles, torn tendons, sprains, dislocated joints, eye infections, ear infections, hair loss, skin cancers, multiple foot issues, black and fungus toe nails, etc.

On request, both women wrote about the toll on their bodies. Their accounts reveal that many years of training and competing in athletic events resulted in extensive catalogues of injury and misadventure. "Expect the Unexpected," Dottie begins:

Races seldom go according to plan and therein lies the reality of sport and at the same time the intrigue and excitement. While training for the Ironman in 1986 I started out to take my last long ride up to visit my parents in northern Vermont. It was about 120 miles of hilly countryside but on a beautiful Fall day. Who could resist that last chance to enjoy a perfect day before leaving for Hawaii? I relished the turning of the leaves, the last of the crops being harvested and the thought of fresh pressed cider at a farm stand.

Two of our sons met me for lunch about two hours from my destination. Some ominous, threatening clouds rolled in, hiding the sun's rays. I decided to put on another layer of clothing as it was getting cooler. The raindrops started falling first and then the rain turned to sleet, and I was very cold. I pushed on.

The next thing I knew I was lying on iced-over railroad tracks in the middle of the road! The pains in different parts of my body were so severe I didn't know which was the worst. My helmet was pulverized to bits, my elbow was a bunch of mush and my hip had a grapefruit hanging off of it. My dad took me to a local hospital, but it was immediately clear that I had to get back home to a major medical center for surgery. The diagnosis: fractured elbow in fifty pieces, concussion, fractured hip and road rash. I sent a telegram the next day to my friends in Hawaii: "Enjoy your breakfast and please—crack eggs, NOT bones."

Ironman triathlon posed other physical challenges for Dottie:

They always had very good medical help. I had hyponatremia one time. I kept drinking but had depleted sodium and potassium.

But Ironman triathlon was not responsible for all of Dottie's physical ailments.

The continuing saga in the pursuit of sporting excellence bedeviled us with a lifetime of skin cancers. As teenagers and beyond, we slathered ourselves with iodine and baby oil and sunbathed, often making silver foil reflectors to get greater tans. As years went by, we started seeing strange little "popups" where nothing but smooth skin had previously existed. Then, suddenly, brown spots were arriving unannounced on various parts of my body. Now, in old age, a child makes the comment, "If you get enough of those, you'll be tanned all over." The dermatologists love us!

One asks, "Why do we do this?" "Because we love what we do until we can't do it anymore."

Concluding, Dottie explains that the physical costs:

are a part of life in sports and many other activities, depending on the level of competition. There are risks in all activities, even taking a bath. Some accidents are sudden and not always our fault. A huge banner picturing a lion and a lion tamer hung in our garage, which said, "Be Alert and You Won't Get Hurt." Well, none of us wants to get hurt and we take all possible precautions to prevent accidents and injury.

My "battle scars," mostly from bike accidents, left me with a picket fence on my collarbone, scars from a fractured elbow repair, a knee with no cartilage, skin cancer excisions, etc. When I was going to a department store to buy a fancy dress for a gala, I was very specific that my left shoulder had to be covered. The salesperson tried her best to assist me with my request. She brought in an armful of clothes and I proceeded to try some on. Finally, she said, "You must try on this one." I reluctantly did as I was told. Actually, I was so happy to even have a salesperson I tried it on. I noticed the salesperson glance at my left collarbone with rather wide eyes and possible tears in her eyes. My secret was OUT! She stared at the "Picket Fence" of my clavicle, the result of at least three fractures from bike accidents.

The most dramatic fall from fame came after I started rowing. I set a world record at the 2015 [*Concept2 Indoor*] Rowing World Championship in the 80–84 age group. Alas, standing on the awards stage radiant with a victory, I took a step backwards falling off the stage with a winners' engraved hammer in hand. I fell four and a half feet to the floor below, landing on the handle of the hammer. My good friend who viewed this disaster almost got sick. The E.R. verified I had fractured, again, my clavicle, and torn my hamstring. Those severe injuries did not turn a traditional black and blue but a pure coal black that spread to an entire chest and a leg limb.

Uncharacteristically Celeste's list of injuries and ailments is linear and chronological, further emphasizing the remoteness of the subject from the story she wanted to tell:

1982—I had Colin's flu when I started Grandma's Marathon in Duluth. I did not feel well after five miles. I finished in 4:02 with 107-degree temperature. I was a star at hospital. They did not have many heat stroke victims in Duluth. Then they discovered it was the flu.

1985—I was running around City Park near my parents' in New Iberia, Louisiana, and slid on some seashells. Concussion. Hospital. My mother made me run with their phone number on my shirt after that.

1987—Coming fast on my bike down Bear Creek Canyon one afternoon in November, with the sun behind me, a car approached with his turn signal on. I thought, "He cannot turn in front of me. I cannot stop on this scree." But he did turn—just in front of me. My bike turned parallel, I thought, "How cool is this?" Then I slid down. The bike came out of my clips like skis and missed the car. The driver saw me too late and was shaken. I got up and finished my ride but was afraid to go downhill for ten years.

1989—Once my bike wheel got caught in an expansion joint. I woke up with an ambulance there. I broke my collarbone, but I raced Bolder Boulder [*a very popular 10K fun run*] in a brace a few weeks later.

1980s—There were jellyfish in Kona, and I had a few stings each time.

1998—I was training for Ironman on Highway 63 in Boulder, when I was knocked down by a prairie dog. I remember seeing the wheel wobble and thinking, "I hope this doesn't hurt." And I woke up and the ambulance was there [*again*]. I spent four days in hospital because I broke some ribs and punctured a lung. I made the papers, but I did not make Ironman or the World Championships at Lausanne.

2006—In February I broke my other collarbone in Boulder after stopping to talk on the phone. I got down on my aero bars but missed one bar. Rita picked me up. I would not go to hospital until I bathed and ate. I drove myself home but almost fainted. Dick took me to Emergency at the hospital. And I took a board meeting call for USAT along the way. The doctor says, "It looks bad, but if you're careful it will knit." He saw me each month but finally he said I needed surgery. I said I had to wait until after a bike race in June. He looked at me and said, "Tell me about the bike race. From where to where?" I said, "From San Diego to Annapolis." He just kept looking at me. He couldn't understand. The Race Across America [*Celeste's second attempt*] was great. Lark Birdsong was with me and we had a driver with a long Santa Claus beard. And we won. We won on skill. That was exciting. I had surgery when I got back.

2008—I did Race Across America again. On the first night of the race, I got caught in another expansion joint and flipped over and re-broke my collarbone. I made a figure eight bandage out of a tee shirt and carried on. The doctor with us said, "Are you going to quit?" I said "No." It was fine when I was riding but hurt when I stopped. At Annapolis, we packed up, and Colin and I went to see my daughter Kelly. I had a grandchild being born while I was on the ride. It hurt when I held the baby.

2010—In 2010, I was looking for someone to do the Race Across America with Lark again. I ended up doing Race Across the West with Ann Lantz, a phenomenal rider, Julie Lyons and Susan Griffin-Kaklikian. It took one day and something. We did very well. Very, very well. We set a record. Julie and Ann tried to go after other records. Ann had an accident and spent a year in a halo. It was traumatic for her, but she and Julie did Race Across America two more times and won both times.

2016—On December 26, I was hit by the barrier arm gate of a closed neighborhood. A truck hid it from view. It hurt badly across my chest and I had concussion. I am told that I told two women my husband's name and called 911. I do not remember any of that. I was taken by helicopter to Ft. Myers Trauma Hospital for the night. I had a rainbow colored face for a couple of weeks. Nothing was broken but I had severe pain from whip lash. I fell a month later off my bike on a busy road. The sun was in my eyes. I was riding on a white line but did not know that it had crumbled away on the side. I bounced back up and got back on the bike. I was riding with a guy and did not want to be a baby. Two weeks later I fell and had horrific lumbar pain. Finally, my dog Henry pulled me, and—from standing—I fell and hit my forehead on the ground. So it was a quiet spring.

While Celeste's memoir alludes to just a handful of these challenges, and only in passing, she does make repeated mention of an uncomfortable physical reality that she and many women triathletes confront as they come to grips with the sport. She also repeats the advice she offered to CWW members:

I guess here is where I explain the towel thing. They asked about peeing. I told them that they had to pee. Men pee indiscriminately. I told them to bring a towel and place it on top of their transition gear at the race. Then sit on the towel as they changed from swim gear to bike shoes—standing only causes a Charley horse in spite of what the pros do—or when they changed from bike shoes to run shoes. They howled. But every once in a while, someone will post on FB or jet me an email as to how she thought of me as she used her towel. Almost two decades later. My claim to fame.

However, getting past EEUUWWW was then and is now one of the barriers for non-athletic women flirting with triathlon. "You don't think those geese and that dog are not peeing in this lake?" I'd say, giving another option. "Go ahead."

As I reflect on the extent to which my interventions contributed to the production of stories about their bodies, I conclude that Dottie and Celeste do not position physical transformation as central to the personal metamorphoses they describe. Their memoir narratives remain mostly silent about their bodies until their age puts them at odds with a sporting landscape that favors the appearance and capabilities of younger bodies—male and female.

Dottie and Celeste respond to the physical and cultural constraints brought on by age in different ways. Slipping between first and second, even third, person Dottie muses:

All of us come from "The Factory" with varying body parts, some good, some maybe not so good. In other words, we may choose an activity which utilizes our best body parts, i.e., we develop strong legs perhaps for running or we have a larger build which would lend itself to football or weight events, or being a smaller build and wiry perhaps gymnastics, or ballet. Today, as a senior citizen, I feel strongly that any activity, especially one you love, is beneficial for fitness, diet control, and maintaining maximum health. As we look around us the alternative doesn't look good.

Recently I was a participant in a presentation about training and injuries. Since I had just turned eighty someone suggested I could talk about "Staying alive." Perhaps that is true, but I think the alternative is not good so I prefer to look at how we, senior citizens, can live and have happy, healthier, stronger lives.

The best way not to get injured is to prevent injury in the first place. This requires that you know your body and "Listen to Your Body." Be flexible and change workout plans when necessary. This is often easier said than done. More mature persons need to do stretching and weight work because that is what we lose as we age. Today there are so many opportunities and a great variety of fun stuff like yoga, pilates, Zumba, "Step" and on and on. Online and video options are out there: just select your activity and an appropriate level.

Aging athletes who achieved their personal best times in earlier athletic challenges and begin to decline with age, often give up because they keep comparing their earlier yardstick to where they are now. When you reach your peak and can no longer reach that peak and going down the other side you've got to deal with it. My attitude is just go out and give your best effort on the day and be happy with it.

Triathlon and other sports are good as you get older. When the time comes that you can't run as you did because you've got back problems, or your knees, etcetera, you've got other things you can do. Swimming is a wonderful sport because it uses all the muscle groups and it's great cardio-wise. It doesn't put pressure on the knees. Biking uses different muscle groups as well. You've also got to consider time, when you're older. When you're younger and get stressed, you recover faster. One time I did three triathlons in a weekend, but I can't do that all the time. I look back and get philosophical about things.

When I am working out in an anaerobic way, either in a class or on my own, many spectators make comments or shake a finger at me: "You are going to have a heart attack if you keep that up," or better still, "You better be careful at your age!"

One of the most common questions is: "Do you ever have aches and pains?" And I reply, "The day I don't have aches and pains I'm dead." I can't help but think how many older friends are gone and thank God I'm still here.

The other day I was jogging on the beach and was going slowly enough that I spotted a shark's tooth by the water's edge. I realized it felt good to be upright, putting one foot in front of the other, and enjoying a beautiful day. Amen. When we "Descend" it's really the beginning to feeling good about ourselves and taking advantage of and making every day a great day.

With her body slowing down Dottie looked for other ways to experience and express the freedom she gained by challenging convention. Indoor rowing is a relatively recent addition to her repertoire, and the 80–84 age group world record set in 2015 an impressive new entry on her resume. But indoor rowing represents variation on the theme of athletic endeavor. In a seemingly much greater departure, Dottie belatedly took up painting. She finds synergies between art and sport:

Athletics and art tie in together nicely. I came from an artistic family. My mother was artistic, and my brother, too. He started out painting by number in commercial instruction books. We didn't really have an opportunity to study art. I always wanted to pursue art, but I didn't have professional training, just what they taught in school arts and crafts, which I got from Mum as a home economics teacher. When I got to Jacksonville, I took an art course with Allison Watson; I called her the Swamp Lady because she did swamp water scenes. At first, I was really hesitant. It took a long time before I got started. My first real painting was a birthday present for my husband. I painted all his favorite things. It turned out to be nice and he was pleased.

I started doing realist paintings in acrylics but decided I really had to do something else. I wanted to do abstracts and asked Paul Ladnier. He's now a professor emeritus with UNF. I love the freedom, the color; I love the mystery of not knowing how exactly a painting will turn out. I

In 1999, George celebrated his 70th birthday with a fun run at the beach. George wore number 1 on his race bib, and Dottie wore number 2 (courtesy Pablo Rivera).

love it because I can use oil, and things in my mind can come out. People started seeing my paintings. I did paintings for not-for-profit organizations. I had a show recently with sixty-nine paintings and had one at St John's Cathedral. When we do cruises, I take all my paints (acrylics), flat canvases and wood. For all the crew that help us out on the ship, I have an opening of all my paintings, and give them to the crew. One hairdresser wanted some scissors. I took a landscape I like, then traced scissors, and then turned it into a person—legs, arms and little heart. It was one of the cutest paintings. Someone wanted New York. They'd only seen it from the ship. I loved it so much I had trouble giving it away. You can never do the same painting again. Now I know not to give away a painting I love.

So many people say, "I can't believe you sit and paint for so long." Well first I don't sit; I get up and look around. And when you paint, you get endorphins. It correlates neatly to sports. One time, early one morning, my husband got up and left on a trip. Next thing I knew, it was dark out. I had forgotten about everything else. It's nice to do something later in life. I hear people say, "I would like to do that." It's been a wonderful part to complement all my active things. It's quieter but active: the mind is active; the body is active.

Painting enriches my life in many, many ways.

It is only after reading Dottie's comments about art many, many times that I finally think I understand the complementarity to which she points, and where it fits in terms of her memoir. I suspect it is unintentional, but she uses the same words to express her feelings about art, Ironman triathlons and the boardroom. She alludes to the unknown, but this time the unknown is tied to mystery not fear. She knows that the unknown holds possibilities—the freedom to find potential within, to create her own outcomes, to be able to "change the culture of things." And she anticipates realization of those possibilities with relish. She values that freedom in both art and sport and hopes that others may experience it and realize their unknown potential as well.

Dottie and Celeste both seek freedom, but in old age Celeste once more feels constrained and unfree. In her memoir, Celeste responds to the passage of time by raising and answering three questions: what have I gained? what impact have I had? and what now? In the process of addressing the latter, she finally says something about her body:

My husband, an accomplished athlete himself, was remarkably supportive—with the long hours of training, with the many travels to races, and with the expensive gear. My children were as well, mainly because I

In 2014 Dottie won the 80–84 age group in the world indoor rowing championships. Her art studio doubles as a home gym and, not surprisingly, boasts an indoor rowing machine (courtesy Bob Self and *Florida Times-Union*).

began this departure from normal motherhood when they were four, six and seven. This life is what they knew. Interestingly, there was a trickle down effect.

Tim remained unmoved.

Colin's been my closest ally. When I did triathlon at Denver he wanted to come. And I said, "You have to get up at four," and he said, "OK." He saw me come out of the water and said, "Oh, Mom, you're doing great."

Colin began to risk and try new things. I remember once I raised my eyebrows, not an easy task: they are quite thick. He had just told me he was going to sky dive. "It's dangerous," I said. "*You* are talking to *me* about *dangerous*?"

My largest influence was on my daughter, a major surprise because she spent about three of her four and a half decades playing at fisticuffs with me.

One year I decided to run the LA marathon because Kelly was working there and I thought, like Judy always did, I would combine a trip to see a child along with a tad of athleticism.

Beyond Triathlon

We stayed in a hotel at the start line and spent the day before the race picking up my packet. All afternoon we ran into kiosks advertising a fun run, at that time an oxymoron. It was a 5K that started just after the marathon itself. Kelly had been the South Dakota, Washington State, and Colorado 5K high school record breaker. The pressure was a lot for her, with all our moves. She was three times the new girl at school. What does a girl, new or old, want from school? Friends. How do you keep making friends? Beat the shit, excuse me, out of each and every candidate. As it turned out, she blew the state championship qualifier so she could have a date for the prom, resulting in her being the only one on the team not to get an award from the coach at Awards Night. So when she went off to CU, she quit cold turkey.

"Wouldn't you like to run the 5K while you wait for me?" I'd say each time one of those booths appeared.

"No." The bottom lip protruded, switchblade.

This conversation times three.

And then: "I'm not ready yet."

The morning of the race as we were preparing to go downstairs so I could line up with, get this, the elite—I could do 8-minute miles—I said, "I know what you mean."

"What do you mean?"

"Your father, your brothers, your friends. Everyone knows what I am doing today. If I do not do well, they will know that too. This is a big risk for me. It would be safer for me to have stayed at home."

The lip again.

On the way down the stairs, she said: "I wonder if I have time to sign up for the 5K?"

"Give your purse to the concierge and go!"

And she has been running for fun ever since. Been twenty years. She did a race not long ago with her only training that of pushing a jogging stroller. Seven minute miles. "What could I have done had I really practiced?" she exclaimed.

I feel good when I think of those two moments. So maybe that is a good thing.

But at around age seventy, the wheels fell off the bus.

There was a total knee replacement just before my sixty-ninth birthday. A doctor told me that I had a necrosis—I knew enough Greek not to get out the dictionary—and that I should not, no way Jose, run again. So I did what any triathlete would do. I found another doctor. This one kept me in business for about another five years, and then he heard the skid marks. It was time. I did not argue. Besides, the pain was intolerable, and I would have settled for just walking. As it was, I looked Special Needs.

Then, in the winter, I got very sick with what turned out to be pneumonia and diverticulitis. The weight of the new knee was now balanced by the extraction of a foot of colon.

Dick broke his wrist about the same time. Together, we were one hurt locker.

While Dick continued to worry about what he expected to be his last business hurrah, I soon took stock of my condition:

My brain. I needed a re-boot. The children were beginning a riff that went on about my inability to focus. Or to concentrate.

My body cried for renewal. The fifteen minutes a day of exercise, or a swim or a bike and the prescribed twice a week one mile run were not enough to replace muscle that had begun to desert me.

I was a shell of my former self. I was 22 years younger than my father who outmaneuvered me on both counts within ten minutes of getting out of bed. I had no idea what to do about either. But as I sat there thinking about how to begin to rejoin my bits from head to toe, I remembered a day—about, oh, seventeen years ago—when my world fell apart yet came together, an assonant accordion.

And so, at the age of seventy I decided that I'd had enough of sitting out the game. The short version of the rest of that year is:

A nanny for me, sent by Kelly. Zayda, a former Sandinista who got political asylum in 31 days thirty years ago, had been doing odd jobs around the DC area and one day found herself sleeping in her car. Kelly had known her for a long time. We took her in, and then we had a caretaker and the caretaker had a home.

I signed up for an Ironman distance relay race—this, in Atlantic City. I would ride 112 miles. Two friends would complete the team: a swimmer and a marathoner. We agreed that our goal was to have half a year of working out for a purpose. There was no grandmasters prize. All we had to do is finish in time so the next person could finish in time so the runner could get across the line by midnight.

So I had, at age seventy one, that race to look forward to, to sharpen me, to distinguish me from the other women who walk in the mall for whom the idea of exploration does not occur. I just had to get used to the new self I keep becoming.

I had my luminosity tests to take. I was at 99 percentile brain power index for my age group, but I have slipped to 98.3. I needed to do the tests when I had plenty of quiet time.

Beyond Triathlon

I had a three year stint as coffee chairperson for the Colorado Steering Committee's part in the Leadership Conference at Harvard Divinity School. Those people think I am so clever that the head flew down to meet me in New York in May when I went to Emma's Grandparents Day. That she is coming to meet me instead of asking me to fly to Boston is worth some attention. I would not be who I am, a woman people fly to see, were it not for the skills I learned toeing the start line on a beach on a cold dark morning just before dawn.

Triathlon has taught me about goals, that goals provide the electricity to turn on your light. Funny. It took me a while to realize that I, in the first place, *needed*, that light.

I also have the chance to act as a friend. Rita got a knee replacement. Heidi's breast cancer has spread. These are people who have been there for me. Triathlon taught me how to be a friend. One would think such a thing would come naturally.

No. I needed hours and hours of physical depletion alongside a partner and a bike path to learn what is a friend and how to be one.

I have learned who I am. And where I end and someone else begins and to honor the space in between.

I am grateful.

Celeste's various accounts reveal that this cycle of restless reflection followed by frantic goal setting, continues into the present. It is as if she keeps choosing a narrative trail that loops back around to somewhere on the path behind her, failing to recognize the trail head when she comes across it again. The next time round led to Celeste's participation in the Alcatraz Swim in 2015. That was the day I first met her. In a recent addition to her memoir Celeste writes:

In the sixties there was a ballad by—was it Petula Clark?—with the refrain "I've seen the world from both sides now."

That was this past weekend for me.

I had flown in last Friday from my 98-year-old father's—from my origin as helpless Southern woman—with an impressive bandage and six stitches giving the travelers at DIA something to gape at. I am, after all, an old woman. But this was just another sports injury.

Zayda and I are waiting at the local Doc in the Box, for me to have said stitches removed. "Wasn't I here before?" I asked Zayda as she executed a U-turn on Colorado Blvd, waving at the jaws of death.

"Yes. Yays. Lass year. When you fell off Ms Kelly's boys' rolling thing in the basement and you crashed into the wall."

"I remember."

So one characteristic of the past forty years has, indeed, been emergency room visits. Downside. The upside has been the *sine qua non* of a life well lived. To wit: Goals and the recipe by which to achieve them.

I have learned I can do anything I want to do. The New York Marathon in 1980 in which few women participated, taught me that.

I have learned to departmentalize fear and carry on. The jump off the ferry into the frigid, shark infested waters of San Francisco Bay and the subsequent swim to Golden Gate Bridge taught me that.

I can equate difficult hit-the-wall moments in my marriage with the fourth quarter of any long-distance event.

This weekend I volunteered to help women help themselves by overcoming the obstacles that confine them. We were to be the Ironman Boulder Swim Finish Volunteers, matching plastic bags to the numbers on the dazzled swimmers after they came out of their 2.4-mile swims. Why were 1,400 people participating in this event? Many were trying to race well enough to get a chance to compete at Kona. Been there, done that. Three times.

The next day, former triathlete friend Rita came over for a few minutes. She is thinking of buying a new bike. At seventy. In fact, our friend Heidi is seventy and did not finish. Another friend is sixty-three and did not qualify so in five months' time will try again in Cozumel.

SO I am in wonder. What we did as a dare leads them to the Holy Grail. Or is it the Holy Grail?

What happens when you need to stop?

I still exercise daily.

I have no races lined up, but I am doing three long events. In July I will swim 1.2 miles in a Colorado lake, planning forty minutes. Sometime in August, friends and I will ride up to the top of Pikes Peak—14,000 feet. And I have signed up for the N.Y.C. Marathon, asking if I can change to the half marathon. To do so, I want to bring my effort to 11 to 12-minute miles. I once ran 7 minutes 45 seconds for ten miles, and 7-minute miles for three miles.

But beyond that?

I did not want to be THAT woman, heralded and photographed for being the oldest out there.

Dottie's memoir provides a clue as to why Celeste struggles to adapt to active old age:

This is NOW: Put aside all of yesteryear and hear an Old Ditty give the "real scoop."

When children visit they examine the refrigerator, taking out each

The continuing cycle of goal setting led to Celeste competing in the Race Across America for a third time in 2008, aged 65. Here, Colorado Sportscaster Marcia Neville (left) interviews Celeste and her team members (left to right: Carol Whipple, Lark Birdsong, Celeste, Helena Harman) (courtesy Marcia Neville).

food package, cartons of liquid, salad dressing, and just about everything, even canned goods. They examine the expiration date very carefully. Great exclamations come forth if an outdated food item is found!

When clerks and other staff started calling me "Madam" or "Ma'am" I knew I was old. At first, I found this offensive but in the South I have come to accept this as a most polite gesture and a compliment to good manners.

It's an adventure when going to a department store for clothing. The salesperson immediately leads me over to "Full" figure fashion, is it really fashion? Even though I'm old, do they recognize I am a size six? Then I go to Junior sizes with "thong" underpants and micro tops meant for teenagers. The nightgown department offers me a flannel nightgown down to my ankles in a flowery Early American print. Do they think that decades-old husbands want their wives, no matter the age, NOT to look sexy and alluring?

Celeste (middle row, fourth from right, wearing her medal and red gloves) and 2008 Race Across America team "Colorado Flash," with their support crew after completing the event, won the over 50 female category (courtesy RAAM).

Today I have with me at most times my iPod, iPhone, iPad and computer. Now, why are older folks underestimated as to their abilities? We can all learn. It just takes us a little longer. And if parents or grandparents want to communicate with their children or grandchildren they better "bone up" because if you try and call their home phone [*land line*] they will find it is disconnected and MUST call their cell phones. Most of all we have flashy carrying cases for all equipment.

Going in for a car repair or a new car—be prepared. It's a game we play to cut to the chase and get the facts you need and not all the B.S. rolling forth. One day I was looking for a new car and saw a brilliant, snazzy red coupe in the showroom that looked like it might just fill my bill. However, when the salesperson came over to me and saw "old" me in my rather grubby running clothes he passed me off to another salesperson. The more mature and very friendly salesperson immediately took my bike out of my car and neatly fit it into the potential new car. Bingo. A perfect fit and the "Sold" sign was put on the dashboard.

FEELS....SO GOOD!!
NAPLES, FLORIDA
April 8 2019

Many times, life seems to be about setting goals....and achieving them....or not!, and then resetting them. Certainly in sports.... and in so many area of our busy lives.... Down here in In Florida, bike rides always have goals, a better avg. speed than before.....a longer ride than last week....lower heart rate ....more power... and it always makes you feel great when it's over......and you achieved your goal. This young lady set a goal in this year's Pan Florida ride to complete the entire 200 mile course....well, she did... and she very loudly yelled..."Feels So Good"!!!

18" x 24"

The deal was done with provision that if the previous salesperson (who would not wait on me) got one cent from the sale, it was off. I got the car and, sorry to say, a few speeding tickets followed.

When the more regal Iron Ladies went to races, the young "bucks" came over to see our bikes. Triathletes are known for a lot of stuff. The observers had eyes popping out of their heads because we had state of the art everything. They always asked, "How come you have all this state of the art everything?" and my reply, "Because at our age we need every advantage we can get."

Dottie acknowledges more overtly than Celeste that with their advancing years they ventured into another valley, one that is separated from the sporting landscape due to age. Celeste and her triathlon friends appear to set goals and expectations consistent with those they set when they were younger, when they were middle-aged. After a struggle, Celeste seems to acknowledge—possibly even to accept—the need to modify those goals as her body ages. But it still seems to irk. If her modest achievements are celebrated on the basis of age they are no longer about "stepping up" as a woman. Recognized as an old woman she is constrained thrice; by a resistant body; by deeply embedded conventions that still tend constrain female athletic agency in barely visible ways; and by cultural conventions that do not cast the aged and aging as athletes, as constructive participants in the world of sports.

Dottie and Celeste were at odds with convention when they first started along their roughly parallel athletic paths. They did so just as magazines and major sports labels across the globe began to sell the image of the young, fit woman. The body-less memoirs affirm that their underlying point is not about physical transformation. Instead the narratives reveal that Dottie and Celeste stand for a vision of sport as radical action for women. Through this radical action they transformed themselves, other women, and—in part—the sport of triathlon.

But age presents another challenge. Dottie and Celeste only write about their bodies when the subject has a purpose. As a token athlete once more, Celeste's conundrum is evidence both of how much has changed in the world of sport and how much remains unaltered. It is a reminder that the memoirs do not celebrate a job well done. The culture of sport

Opposite: While ambivalent about being the token old woman, Celeste participated in the 2019 Pan Florida Challenge. The surge of satisfaction she felt on completing the event, led her to yell, "Feels so good" and to seek a permanent reminder of the moment in the form of a painting by artist Michael Kilburn (courtesy Michael Kilburn, 18" × 24" oil on canvas). Communicating with Kilburn about the event, Celeste explained, "Many times, life seems to be about setting goals ... and achieving them ... or not!, and then resetting them. Certainly in sports ... and in so many areas of our busy lives... Down here in Florida, bike rides always have goals, a better avg. speed than before ... a longer ride than last week ... lower heart rate ... more power ... and it always makes you feel great when it's over ... and you achieved your goal."

has not yet shifted to fully involve, accommodate and reflect the presence and constructive contributions of women, particularly women who are not young. As the final pages drafted by Dottie and Celeste reveal, this is, in part, the problem at the heart of the memoir project.

Conclusion:
The Anticipation Contained
in April

To the very end, the over-riding aim of the memoirs remains partially concealed in the light and shadow of the respective narratives constructed by Dottie and Celeste, even as they attempt to draw some conclusions.

Dottie's final paragraphs continue to focus on experiences of aging. She strikes a positive note, identifying those things she values in the present—family, friends, and the experiences shared with them.

This "Old Dittie's" grand finale would make mention of the most significant and most positive aspects of being an "Old Dittie."

Let's start with "Then" and proceed to "Now."

A blink of the eye and there's an empty nest. Perhaps no one is ever ready because you just don't think it will ever happen. Retirement was probably our least planned-for event. First, how could WE possibly be that old? Do we look that old? What to do now? No hobbies and you are really in trouble. No social interactions and you'll be all alone. My rule upon my husband's retirement was, "For breakfast and for dinner but never for lunch." It's an adjustment for sure. No matter what perfect appearing families might say, we believe, "Every family is dysfunctional to some degree." So we soldier on and find the most positive aspects of "old Ditties."

We share so many wonderful times together and get into an understanding routine which is satisfying to both of us. We look forward to each day in a different light. Appreciating a different routine from the early years' craziness. A routine more relaxed, i.e., reading the newspaper, leisurely, with a cup of coffee. He reads three newspapers every day and does crosswords (always in ink since "he's not an amateur"), works out when he can, sometimes just physical therapy. I have daily workouts. I work out six days a week with friends, especially Kitty. I played tennis with her Mom for decades, and then did triathlons with her daughter for decades.

My, what a contrast to those early years! Appreciating the early morning darkness, awaiting chirping birds, the beginning sounds of morning traffic and the sun just beginning to peek over the trees while the darkness fades with the brightening dawn. A day deciding how we will spend it, aside from a Physical Therapy appointment or a Board meeting. I also have painting and many activities. Wonderful choices. Sunsets bring a romantic setting to another meaningful day. Finally, a day comes when you can make "Free choices" and not fret about it or feel guilty.

We travel, we share good times with family; we appreciate the beauty of every day and the goodness God has given us. We love to travel and continue to take advantage of many opportunities. It goes without question that we first support family members at their events, no matter if sport, school performances or special celebrations, anywhere in the world. Travel is an education and broadens our perspective on people and the world.

I think we have a closeness that comes with age and a long life together. At our recent "165th Birthday," his eighty-fifth and my eightieth, we had two hourglasses printed on the tee shirts given to all our friends. The hourglasses had the sand almost running through on George's and a little over two-thirds of the way on mine. We celebrated with a run/walk on the sandy beach, enjoyed healthy food, live music from a favorite Quintet and photos of everyone. We were both more than happy that the sand was still running.

A positive aspect to "Aging Up" is the confidence to go with gut feelings. In early years you pass on gut feelings because you hesitate to trust your instincts. Today we both usually say in unison, "Does it pass the smell test?" This is especially useful in critiquing news reports. And we are usually right to be skeptical.

As sand continues to run through "our" hourglass, it brings to mind how your life becomes more meaningful with different priorities—one becomes more "Regal" and not "Old." When your mind is cleared of a chockfull agenda 24/7 there is suddenly an awakening to focus on different levels of attention. As more mature adults it is easier for us to prioritize. In the hectic early years, we attend to the most pressing crisis of the moment. Now we know what's important to us and attend to our list in orderly fashion.

Remember in school or even college when a classmate would make a remark to you, maybe about what you were wearing or "too bad you didn't get invited to that overnight"? Well, that really stung, and it was very upsetting. Now it doesn't matter because you have matured, and most remarks of a superficial nature don't hit a target anymore. All that is over. Celebrations of aging up can be very special with gatherings of family and friends in whatever way one chooses. It's easy to find a reason for reunion: birthday, anniversary, weddings, baby birth, new home, renewed vows, etc. The Girl Scout saying applies here, "Make new friends but keep the old: One is Silver the other Gold!" We are very happy and grateful to be "Golden Oldies."

In these remarks, Dottie's sporting life and her work to enhance female sporting opportunities are not completely removed to a distant, forgotten past. Among the reflections are references to board meetings, and to physical therapy appointments, travel to sporting events, and having quality sport equipment. And once more Dottie talks about freedom, the freedom to choose. A persistent refrain, Dottie regularly gestures toward it, like a landmark seen from different points along the trail. But that is not where the narrative trail ends.

It is Celeste who directs her readers' vision finally from the shadowy undergrowth to the stunning panorama of the metaphorical landscape through which we have traveled:

I am at my desk this mid spring morning, which, in Colorado transcribes to glaring sunlight and dust. We need rain. "April is the cruelest month," said T.S. Elliot, "Mixing memory and desire."

Bear with me; Milne said of Pooh, "Eating honey is a very good thing to do. But there is a moment just before you begin to eat it that is better than when you are." This anticipation contained in April matches the spirit of same.

It matches the feeling of where we are in this tome.

We have a lot left to do. A recent world event, in the United States, showcased how far behind we remain. The Boston marathon winner was an American. On paper. He was Kenyan. But that an American had won in x many years seemed so much more important than mentioning the name of the female winner who turned in a blistering record of 2:11. We had to search in the small print in the back of the papers to find her name and stats.

In the boardroom, women are still honeys or dolts. The female secretarial work takes a lot of, excuse me, shit. Of course, there are honeys and dolts in both genders. But the men fifty-five years and over must be re-wired or else die off. For what awaits, they are not prepared.

Conclusion

Women still say, "I could never do that." They still hide behind the shame of not being able to keep up on a bike ride or at a swim, and so they do not show up. What this means is our job is not yet done. We could not have possibly already hit all the women who finished their proper schooling before Title IX. So they still come trickling in.

While twenty years ago, these women came in with their daughters, now their daughters are bringing them. They are not all stay at home mothers now. They are airline pilots, gynecologists, stockbrokers—and exercise and what comes with it is a required balance to their lives.

For our first open water swim this year, on the Saturday morning at the pond, there occurred a scene that happily sums the story. We had twenty-five women with their pink swim caps. The gravel pond where we swim is anything but. It is about three quarters of a mile across, and wide. It is very hard to sight anything. Now there is a slight change, some building going on more than a mile away. About 350 yards out is a hidden sandbar, which we use as a stop point for the novices. We have added three buoys, say at 6:00 on a clock. On Saturday mornings triathletes come by the hundreds and swim, but this time the cold June 3 weather kept the crowds away. I expected our women to wade in and do a few dunks and maybe swim five strokes, but they all, even the most timid, swam to the sandbars and back.

Seeing that pack of pink caps fill the lake was indeed for me a proud moment, I had graduated. I had the feeling that this was the pinnacle of my Judy life.

Both Dottie and I can curtsy on the stage of female development since Title IX. We have made great strides in empowering women to empower themselves, empowering them to ask for the equal pay for equal work, to demand a tone of respect and losing the "luv's" and "hon's" in daily workday conversations. We both believe with all our hearts that the chief responsibility of women thinking good about themselves and, thus, demanding that others do likewise, comes with sport and the satisfaction of owning the day when one nails a ten minute mile or learns how to descend Old Stage Road without riding the brakes all the way down. We have used sport as an analogy for life, bringing the skills that got us to a finish line into the boardroom, the bedroom, and a line of gridlocked traffic.

I recall Dottie expressing a similar sentiment about participation in sport having impacts for women beyond sport a day or two before we all met at Naples. Luckily, I recorded the conversation. On transcribing the recording, it feels as though I have reached the final marker on the trail and passed beyond the tree line. I can see the nearby summit for the first time. In the transcript of the conversation, Dottie begins with the connection between triathlon and other sports: "A lot of women who did do triathlon continued on in other sports, as long as they could be active." *After making reference to Title IX, she continues:*

I look at the future, and they have to preserve what they have. They've got to be informed. They've got to be active. We're qualified for everything but look at the legislature and there's no women anywhere. Men should not be making decisions for women in health care. I'm writing letters to say, "We need women on boards." In some Scandinavian countries, half the representation on corporate boards have to be women. You have to fight for that. This generation feels entitled. They don't know how hard we fought to get them equality. Some things can go away. We can't go back to the dark ages.

Now I see.

Dottie and Celeste are not just writing about themselves or for themselves. And they are not just writing about sport.

Dottie and Celeste have shown that participation in sport can empower women with confidence, it can teach them about the extent of their own potential, and the power of setting and achieving goals as a means to realizing that potential. It can release them from the inhibiting bonds of convention and give them the freedom to choose a path for themselves. The process is cyclic. As Celeste put it, she has to "get used to the new self I keep becoming."

But that is not the point of the dual memoir project.

Dottie and Celeste's narratives remind us of the importance of looking beyond the individual journey. The significance of personal journeys can readily be lost, when viewed in isolation. By placing their two journeys together, Dottie and Celeste allow us to see the intersections, the common challenges, and better understand the cultural landscape as a whole. We can see that on their sporting journeys Dottie and Celeste have altered the landscape. Along with other pioneer women triathletes they have carved out the paths along which many more transformed women follow.

But the sport itself and sport in general has not transformed fully. Dottie and Celeste are concerned that the feelings of satisfaction and growing confidence that women gain through participation in sport might stunt the flourishing growth of the spring of opportunity for women. To return to Celeste's theme, it is April. The summer of equality has not yet arrived. Those of us who did not have to battle for sporting opportunities for women might mistake the warmer weather of spring for summer, but Dottie and Celeste know that we are not there yet.

When talking about good health and fitness in the final chapter of her memoir draft, Dottie argues, adding emphasis to particular words along the way:

There are so many great books available on exercise and fitness and diet that I prefer to talk about philosophy or maybe the psychology of what I've learned along the way. I have heard from all walks of life that most folks just want a "Quick Fix" for all of the above mentioned. *There is NO* "Quick Fix," not in becoming "Fit" or losing weight. If it took fifteen years to become obese it will take years to take it off safely and forever.

Wrapping up their memoirs, the suggestion Dottie and Celeste appear to make, is that there is "No quick fix" to gender inequality either. When she writes about the evolution of the nursing profession Dottie underlines the importance of continuity, reasoning that the introduction of change by one generation of pioneers does not represent the end of the process of change. It can take more than a few decades to "change the culture of things" permanently.

The memoirs are not meant simply to tell heart-warming and entertaining tales of personal transformation through sport, or to broadcast the efforts Dottie and Celeste have made to share the keys to transformation with other women.

The real point of the project is this—for sport itself to be transformed and, with it, society more broadly we need to see a far-reaching "change in the culture of things." That transformation may have started, but it is not yet complete. We may delight in the progress that has occurred, but if we are distracted, we will not reach the finish line. Women's sport is still in transition. We have not reached the end point of gender equality.

Books by and for
Women Triathletes

Attwood, Meredith. *Triathlon for the Every Woman: You Can Be a Triathlete. Yes. You.* Da Capo Lifelong Books, 2019.

DiFabio, Alicia. *Women Who Tri: A Reluctant Athlete's Journey Into the Heart of America's Newest Obsession.* Velo Press, 2017

Edwards, Sally. *Triathlons for Women.* Velo Press, 2010.

Hodgett, Debra. *Tri-Mom: Swimming, Biking and Running Through Motherhood.* Dog Ear Publishing, 2013.

Lacke, Susan. *Life's Too Short to Go So F*cking Slow: Lessons from an Epic Friendship That Went the Distance.* Velo Press, 2017

Lacke, Susan. *Running Outside the Comfort Zone: An Explorer's Guide to the Edges of Running.* Velo Press, 2019.

Lindley, Siri. *Surfacing: From the Depths of Self-Doubt to Winning Big and Living Fearlessly.* Velo Press, 2016.

Moss, Julie, and Robert Yehling. *Crawl of Fame: Julie Moss and the Fifteen Feet That Created an IRONMAN TRIATHLON LEGEND.* Pegasus Books, 2018.

Sims, Stacy. *Roar* Rodale Books, 2018.

Tourmina, Sheila. *Swim Speed Secrets for Swimmers and Triathletes* Velo Press, 2013.

USA Triathlon and Tara S. Comer. *The Women's Guide to Triathlon.* Human Kinetics, 2015.

Wellington, Chrissie. *A Life Without Limits: A World Champion's Journey.* Center Street, 2012.

Bibliography

Note about sources: This work draws substantially on memoirs drafted by Celeste Callahan and Dottie Dorion, as well as the recordings and transcripts of multiple recorded conversations conducted with Callahan and Dorion in 2015 and 2017. Below are listed these primary sources and other sources consulted.

Primary Material

Callahan, Celeste. "Contents May Have Shifted." Memoir draft, Denver, 2014. In Jane E. Hunt Private Collection.

Callahan, Celeste. Interview by Jane E. Hunt. August 15, 2015.

Callahan, Celeste. Interview(s) by Jane E. Hunt. May 15–17, 2017.

Callahan, Celeste, and Dorion, Dottie. Joint Interview by Jane E. Hunt. May 17, 2017.

Dorion, Dottie. "Contents May Have Shifted." Memoir draft, Vermont, 2014. In Jane E. Hunt Private Collection.

Dorion, Dottie. Interview by Jane E. Hunt. August 12, 2015.

Dorion, Dottie. Interview(s) by Jane E. Hunt. May 13–15, 2015.

Additional Material

Booth, Douglas. "Escaping the Past? the Cultural Turn and Language in Sport History." *Rethinking History* 8, no. 1 (2004): 103–125.

Curl, Jim. "The US Triathlon Series (USTS) History: 1982–1993." USA Triathlon History Project, 2020. https://www.teamusa.org/USA-Triathlon/About/Multisport/.

Gray, Doug. "Women's Committee Award of Excellence: The Legendary Figures Honoured So Far." International Triathlon Union. May 1, 2018. https://www.triathlon.org/news/article/womens_committee_award_of_excellence_the_legendary_figures_honoured_so_far.

Hawaiian Triathlon Corporation. "Bud Light Ironman Triathlon World Championship XI Race Results." October 14, 1989. http://www.ironman-hawaii.com/ergebnislisten/hawaii/im-hawaii1989.pdf.

International Triathlon Union. "Honorary Members." Last modified February 9, 2017. https://www.triathlon.org/about/honorary_members.

International Triathlon Union Women's Commission. "Canon Triathlon World Championships Women's Conference—Women in Triathlon: Making the Olympic Dream Come True." 1991. Sarah Springman Private Collection.

Bibliography

IRONMAN®. "Brand Guidelines." 2020. https://www.ironman.com/brand-guide
    lines.
Race Across America. 2020. https://www.raceacrossamerica.org/.
USA Triathlon. "Timeline." USA Triathlon History Project, 2020. https://www.tea-
    musa.org/USA-Triathlon/About/Multisport/History.

Index

Index